# The
# Soul
# Purpose

## Unlocking the
## Secret to Health,
## Happiness and Success

Dr. M. Ted Morter, Jr.

Published by
Dynamic Life, LLC
215 W. Poplar
Rogers, Arkansas 72756


Library of Congress Cataloguing-in-Publication Data

Morter, M.T.
    The soul purpose : unlocking the secret to health, happiness and
success / Dr. M. Ted Morter, Jr. — Rogers, Ark. :
Dynamic Life, LLC, 2001.

    ISBN 0-96705084-0-9 (pb.)
    ISBN 0-96705084-1-7 (hb.)
    p. / cm.
Includes index.

    1. Medicine and psychology. 2. Mind and body. 3. Self.
4. Self-actualization (Psychology) I. Title.

R726.5 .M675 2000
613—dc21                    CIP
                            00-108307

Project Coordination by Jenkins Group, Inc.

Printed in the United States of America

03  02  01      •   5  4  3  2  1

*This work is dedicated to the doctors and patients worldwide
that have come or been sent to me
as we all work together to see health return
to countless persons who had all but given up
to the disease process working within them.*

**OTHER BOOKS BY DR. M. TED MORTER, JR.**

Correlative Urinalysis: The Body Knows Best (1987)

Chiropractic Physiology: A Review of Scientific Principles as
Related to the Chiropractic Adjustment with Emphasis on the
Bio Enenergetic Synchronization Technique (1988)

Your Health, Your Choice: Your Complete Personal Guide to
Wellness, Nutrition and Disease Prevention (1990)

The Healing Field:
Restoring the Positive Energy of Health (1991)

An Apple A Day? Is it Enough Today? (rev. 1997)

Exercise or Diet: Which Will Win the Race to Health? (1997)

Dynamic Health: Using Your Own Beliefs, Thoughts and
Memory to Create a Healthy Body (rev. 1997)

# INFORMATION FOR THE READER

The information presented in this book is a compilation of concepts and principles developed by the author during the course of the past four decades. These concepts and principles relate to maintaining and promoting health, not to treating disease or other physical complaints. The reader is specifically cautioned against applying concepts in this book for therapeutic purposes in lieu of professional healthcare. The reader is urged to consult licensed healthcare professionals for diagnosis and treatment of health problems. This book deals with the basic concept that the body functions as a unit, that various elements of lifestyle influence physiology, and that certain concepts and ideas presented are intended to offer suggestions for examining facets of one's lifestyle that can impact physiology. The main purpose of this book is to make the reader aware of the affect of the mind on the physical body.

No guarantee or assurance is given for specific individuals to obtain specific results from the adaptation of any suggestion. Regular professional healthcare examinations are important for early detection and treatment of any disease. This publication deals primarily with prevention of diseases rather than with disease treatment.

Certain persons considered experts may disagree with one or more statements in this publication. However, the author is of the opinion that such statements are based upon reliable, sound report and authority. Nothing stated in this publication shall be construed as an offer of any product for the diagnosis, cure, mitigation, or treatment of any disease.

—Dr. M. T. Morter, Jr.

# TABLE OF CONTENTS

Acknowledgments                                           ix

Introduction                                              xi


PART I  THE PATH OF ENLIGHTENMENT                          1

    Chapter 1: The Powers Within You           3

    Chapter 2: Your Mind Matters              21


PART II  THE PATH OF KNOWLEDGE                            51

    An Introduction to Booster Thoughts        53

    Chapter 3: The Physical Plane             55

    Chapter 4: The Mental Plane               87

    Chapter 5: The Spiritual Plane           139


PART III  THE PATH OF FULFILLMENT                        167

    Chapter 6: Universal Consciousness        169

    Chapter 7: Practical Steps to a Healthier Life    175


Summary of Points                                        201

Endnotes                                                 204

Index                                                    205

# ACKNOWLEDGMENTS

The work that I share with you in this publication is dedicated to my family who has permitted me the time and energy that it has taken over the past months.

Thank you, Anna, for the uncounted hours you have worked with me to see this become a reality. Without you it wouldn't have happened. I have loved watching you grow throughout this task as you studied and wrote and studied some more. Thank you, Tom, Sarah, and Russ for sharing your wife and your mom as we tried to put this material together in an effort to help those less healthy than you.

And Janna, for your help with the cover material. And Ted for your patience and impatience as the work progressed. Your sons, Ted IV, Chuck and Phil, will better see a healthier tomorrow as a result of this understanding.

Help came from everywhere. From Sue, with her age-old wisdom and shared concepts. From Marjorie, my companion these many years. From the whole office staff who contributed in direct and indirect ways to make the way easier. From the patients who sought my help and convinced me that I truly had a method of helping those who could not help themselves. They needed to be shown a better way. They needed to see what they were doing to themselves.

Every part and role was vital. Without each of you the struggle would have seemed insurmountable. The joint effort is what we all needed to see this project come to fruition. We saw that early on and used that format to bring it all together.

But most of all, this material is dedicated to the millions who are still suffering from disease and pain without knowing or realizing that they, too, can benefit from the steps and principles herein shown.

—Dr. M. Ted Morter, Jr.

# INTRODUCTION

> Unless a man can link his written thoughts with
> the everlasting wants of men, so that they shall
> draw from them as from wells, there is no more
> immortality to the thoughts and feelings of the
> soul than to the muscles and the bones.
> —Henry Ward Beecher

Let me ask you a question. Who do you believe is in charge of your health? Is it your doctor, nurse, acupuncturist, herbalist, nutritionist, or you? If your answer is anyone other than you, then what I'm about to say may come as a rude awakening. I firmly believe and *know for a fact* that *you* are in charge of *your* health. So, the first thing we need to address is our beliefs.

When I was about thirteen years old, which would have been 1948, I lived through an experience that changed the direction of my life forever. It all started when my brother Bill had an accident on our Ohio farm. He was in serious trouble when we took him to the local hospital—pale and barely conscious. He didn't respond to the doctor's treatment. He only continued to get worse until the doctor told my father that they were doing everything they could, but that Bill was dying.

My father could not accept the news that his ten-year-old son was dying, so he simply picked him up and started out of the hospital with him. You can probably imagine the scene that took place in that small Ohio hospital that day. It is fair to say that chaos reigned. Nurses and doctors began to scream at my father that he couldn't take Bill out of the hospital, that Bill would die if he left the hospital. My father, bless his soul, turned to them and repeated what they had told him: that Bill was going to die if he *stayed* in the hospital. I'm not sure if Dad knew exactly what he was going to do with Bill when he left the hospital, but I'm certain that his paternal instincts kicked in to save his little boy, if at all possible. He knew he needed an alternative to the standard healthcare.

Upon arriving home, my father called the local chiropractor, who was a well-respected man in our little community. When he heard my father's story, he left an office full of waiting patients to rush to Bill's side. And that's when things got really exciting!

The doctor worked with Bill for quite a while. At the time, I didn't know what he was doing. All I knew was that as the doctor worked on Bill, he began to become more alert and color returned to his face. More impressive yet, after about fifteen minutes Bill was not only better, he was sitting on the floor asking for his toys!

Now, I was only thirteen years old, but I was sharp enough to realize that something very important had just happened. I mean, that chiropractor had just saved my brother's life! I realized at that very moment the significance of this situation. My teenaged brain decided that while we needed doctors like those in the hospital, we also needed doctors like the one who came to our farm and saved my brother Bill. And, under the circumstances, that thought was quite understandable. In reality, that thought set in motion a chain of events that directed my life toward alternative healthcare. It showed me that when the doctors at the hospital said, "There's nothing more we can do," that did *not* mean that there was nothing more that could be done.

You see, I was always an inquisitive boy. I continually took things apart to see how they worked. I asked questions, even if that was not a popular thing to do. Sometimes the answers were not acceptable to me, so I would have to continue to ask more questions. I always wondered what it was that the doctor did for Bill that day. Why had it worked to save him? Was it a miracle? I decided that science must hold the answers to many of my questions. After completing bachelor's and master's degrees in science I still didn't have the answers that I needed, so I went to chiropractic college, hoping to find my answers there. By now I had clarified my early thoughts of age thirteen. Now I realized that what I believed was that it was necessary to have *alternatives* to medicine—other options. I was searching for those alternatives because obviously medicine didn't have all the answers or Bill would have been saved at the hospital.

In the early years of my practice I helped most, but not all, of the patients who came to me. It was the patients who did not respond totally and favorably who sparked my search to understand more. If enthusiasm and a zeal for helping people could do the trick, I would have had the healthiest patients alive. However, I needed to know why some people responded favorably and quickly and others didn't. I knew it was something other than luck and that what I was doing worked for most. I had to find out why it didn't work for all. After thirty-nine years of searching, researching, and working with thousands of patients, I have put together some answers.

Many years ago, I established what I call the "Six Essentials for Life." These six essentials are: what you eat, what you drink, how you exercise, how you rest, what you breathe, and what you think. Everyone has choices in these six essential areas of life. For years I placed almost equal importance on each of the six essentials. Over time, I realized beyond a shadow of doubt, that one of these essentials far outweighs the others in importance—and that is, what you think.

What you think actually governs your life. You are the image of what you think. Your thinking establishes your beliefs, thus it controls your actions, attitudes, personality, and even affects your physical condition. In order to change your life, you must change the way you think. In other words, if you continue to think what you've always thought, you'll continue to get what you've always gotten. We continually think and do something, then hope or pray for a different outcome. That's probably not going to happen. It hasn't happened yet.

Beliefs are based on personal experience—what we see, hear, read, learn from others, and conclude as a result of these experiences. Since these beliefs are learned, not mandated by God or the power you believe built you, then they are man-made and subject to error. At one time people believed the earth was flat. They thought that if they went too far they would just drop off the edge and vanish forever. Now, as we know, the earth never was flat. The earth was as round as it could be, while those inhabiting it thought it was flat. Their belief that it was flat did not make it so, but it certainly influenced their lifestyle. Even though your beliefs control your life, what you believe to be true today may not be what you believe to be true in the future.

What if you've been looking at life the wrong way? Could it be that things are not exactly as you thought they were? Did you ever have a nagging suspicion that some of the fundamental elements of life could be different than most people perceive them to be? Do you have the intellectual freedom to venture out onto less traveled ground?

What if you had more control over your life and health? Join me in a journey, a journey to truth. A journey that will take you beyond belief, to a place where fulfillment comes in "knowing." I will lead you through a new set of beliefs. Based on my experience with thousands of patients over the past thirty-nine years, this belief system has been adopted by people from all walks of life. I have been teaching this system to healthcare professionals for over twenty-five years. Thousands of doctors now follow this system, leading their patients to see things a little differently.

As you read this book you will become enlightened by a way of life that places *you* in control. And, while these seemingly new concepts will be made available to you, it will be up to you to activate them in your own life. I say "seemingly new" because they may be new to you, but these concepts are as old as the universe. If you see this as a journey, then you will realize that I can only lead you so far, then you must go, armed with this new knowledge, through the remainder of your life. While reading this book, you may find some long sought-after answers. You may discover some brand-new questions. Some of your core beliefs may be challenged a little. You may get that "I knew it!" feeling. Or you may find that the things you always believed in are true.

I ask that you have an open mind, a sense of adventure, and a tingling curiosity for what life is all about. In this book I draw from the deep, innate powers that make up the intelligence of the universe—the intelligence that is in every one of us. I believe that our body, mind, soul, and spirit generate an energy that determines who we are. I believe that getting our soul in harmony with God's spirit is the key to a happy, healthy, successful life. I guess you could say I'm a soul man.

My work has shown me that spiritual and emotional stresses are the precursors to *all* physical ailments and diseases. We all share the realm of spiritual and emotional stresses. Fear, loneliness, anger, hate, jealousy, and similar emotions are common to mankind.

I believe that each body has a unique energy field. In fact, I believe that *all living things* have an energy field in and around them. This energy field has been photographed with Kirlian photography. Your field (as I will refer to it) is affected by many things—what you eat, what you drink, how you exercise, how you rest, the air you breathe, and, most importantly, what you think. In other words, the "Six Essentials for Life" have a direct influence on your field. The reason that what you think is the most important of these is that your belief system is determined by what you think. If you eat a perfect diet, sleep soundly for eight hours each night, live in the mountains where the air is pure, don't smoke, drink pure water, walk five miles every day, yet think that life stinks and that you always get a bum rap, you will develop ailments, a disease, depression, or the like. You will not lead a happy, healthy, successful life.

I believe the links between our body, mind, and spirit are so strong that they are actually impenetrable; they cannot be separated. Our being consists of three planes: physical (the body), mental (the mind), and spiritual (the soul and our connection to God). Our health depends on a harmonious, congruent relationship among these three planes. In this book I will describe my understanding of these planes in detail.

People who attend my lectures or seminars range from healthcare professionals to laypeople seeking personal health. I have spoken at license renewal seminars for health professionals, state conventions, the Mayo Clinic, international foundations, national celebrations, and in my own living room to whomever cared to listen. The message is always the same. The common denominator is the desire to better understand true health, happiness, and success and how these can be attained and shared with others.

Our "soul purpose" is to become as one with God's spirit. As I see it, our soul is our own creation. We create our souls with our conscious minds. On the other hand, our spirits are Godly in nature. In addition, our souls and the spirit within us must be in tune, in harmony, for good health to manifest. When we attain a oneness in soul and spirit, the by-product is good health.

There is a power within us that we are not tapping—at least some of us aren't. Miracles in health and life are for anyone, for *everyone*—not just the few you may have read about or seen on television who "got rid of " cancer or whatever health issue that had affected the quality of their lives. My brother Bill does not hold a corner on the market either and he'd be the first to agree. The power to attain and maintain health is already in you; however, your ability to receive and use it might be jammed. You *can* learn how to open your flow of power. While the concepts in this book are vital to helping you locate and identify the cause of your current health condition, it is not intended that you should discontinue your current healthcare.

The first part of this book explains what I have learned in my research, clinical experience, and everyday living. After some very tedious endeavors to learn, I have arrived at some seemingly simple conclusions that may help lead you to a happy, healthy, and successful life.

I will begin, in Part I, by sharing with you an overview of my concepts. In Part II you will be given some short, daily lessons (Booster Thoughts). These thoughts are designed to help you understand how to put the concepts to work for *you*. How to live your life in a happy, harmonious state. How to resonate with the frequency that created you and the universe by simply opening your mind and your heart. The goal of Part III is to tie it all together, to send you out into the world with a new sense of knowingness. A feeling of calm assuredness that you are part of an almighty plan and that you have the power to control your life and the way you fit into the grand puzzle of the universe.

Listen to and think about what you are about to read. If something really strikes a chord within you, put the book down and *think about it*. If you ever get a tingly feeling up your spine to the top of your head, then you will know that you have been enlightened. Throughout my life, each time I found an answer to a long-sought-after question I would get that tingle. Then I would know I had arrived at a "truth."

# PART I

# The Path of Enlightenment

Seek not to understand that you may believe, but believe that you may understand.

—St. Augustine

# CHAPTER 1

# THE POWERS WITHIN YOU

**In the beginning God created the heavens and
the earth.**
—Genesis 1:1

In the beginning there was God's *Word*. He said, "Let there
be light," and there was light. Today, we still have *the Word* and
the opportunity to let it enlighten us. There is, has always been,
and will always be an ultimate power. God, the omnipotent, supreme energy source, is everywhere, all the time.

When I first began to develop my concepts many people
thought I was "way out there," but as time has passed I find some
are coming out to join me in my thinking. Not all the way "out
there" maybe, but they are getting closer all the time. And I wel-
come them with open arms. I believe there is only one truth and
that life is a quest to discover it—or *rediscover* it. Many authors
these days write about mind–body concepts, or about spiritual
healing. I believe there is a lot of truth in many of these writings.

I have read and studied the works of many authors on these
subjects, from manuscripts written hundreds of years ago to docu-
ments that are hot off the press. Since I teach my concepts to so
many people, I have been presented with hundreds of books that
hold concepts similar to mine. People are constantly wanting me
to read this work or that work to get my opinion. I thoroughly
enjoy doing this. In fact, as I read a book or paper I often glean
information that substantiates or clarifies my own work. However, more often than not, it is revealed to me that many of my
concepts are still quite unique. You may read some things that

are a bit foreign to you. My hope is that you discover that your mind is a special gift of power that only *you* can control. I can turn you on to the power, but *you* must turn the power on.

## SOUL PRINCIPLE

*Truth is not introduced into the individual from without, but was within him all the time.*

—Søren Kierkegaarrd

Our society today is a scientific one. If something can't be measured, weighed, and recorded, then it just might not exist. It's put out to pasture in the "faith" arena—the metaphysical. Metaphysics is the branch of philosophy that seeks to explain the nature of being and reality. It is considered speculative, abstract, abstruse, and supernatural, in general. However, improved technology is quickly bringing the metaphysical into the scientific realm. Scientists can now measure and photograph energy fields around the body, fields that, up until recently, were regarded as supernatural possibilities, not probabilities.

Understand that I am a scientist. I have studied science, have college degrees in science, and have even taught science classes. I believe in science. But I also believe that laws of nature exist whether science can prove them, or not. (Remember, people once believed that the earth was flat!) I give much credit to Dr. Valerie Hunt for her determined and unflappable efforts in photographing the energy fields around the body. These energy fields have been the basis for my work for many years and her scientific breakthroughs in this area have given much credibility to my concepts.

Energy fields were always there, even before they could be measured and photographed. The scientific discovery of them did not change them in any way, but what had been in the supernatural realm has now moved into the scientific one. I believed in these energy fields long before they were ever photographed, but it is now much easier to explain and display my work to others.

Keep in mind that I believe God to be the ultimate energy source. Now, I do not profess to be a scholar of the Bible and I am not trying to convince you to become one or to change your religion. I am merely challenging you to evaluate your beliefs—not the beliefs of others, not the beliefs that have been thrown at you since you were small, but *your own beliefs.*

In my opinion, ultimately you must believe in a supreme power. I call that power God. You may call that power whatever you like, as long as you believe in it. You must believe that there is a power, an energy source, that is greater than you. There is a creator of all—a creator of the entire universe established all living organisms and microorganisms. Not only that, the supreme being created a relationship between all these organisms. Plants, trees, fish, birds, humans, grass, cells, bacteria, and plankton have intermingling relationships with one another. You must appreciate that these relationships exist and that they were created by an omnipotent power that is infinitely greater than you. This book is intended to force you to think about this ultimate power, whatever you may call it, and its grand design—a design that encompasses you, as well as every other organism in the universe. Think about what *you* think about it. Evaluate what you *really* believe, because what you believe, you *become.* This will have the most dramatic impact on your life.

Here are some thoughts and questions that are common to many of us.

> Is my disease caused by lack of medication?
> Does my lifestyle affect my health?
> Is someone or something else in charge of my life?
> What does it really mean to think, "Jesus is my savior"?
> Has my savior arrived on earth yet?
> How should I pray?
> How do I know if my prayers have been answered?
> Is there a difference between my soul and my spirit?
> Where is my spirit?
> Where is God?
> What happens to my soul and my spirit when I die?
> What does God have to do with my health?
> What does it mean to say, "It's God's will"?
> How do thoughts affect my health?
> Do my thoughts affect God?

If you would like the answers to any or all of these questions, read on. The purpose of this book is to enlighten you, to challenge you to think about what you truly believe, to empower you, and to encourage you to reach a higher level of consciousness.

# Introducing Soul and Spirit

> Everything here, but the soul of man, is a passing shadow. The only enduring substance is within. When shall we awake to the sublime greatness, the perils, the accountableness, and the glorious destinies of the immortal soul?
> —William Ellery Channing

As I see it, we each have a soul and a spirit—two separate entities. As I explain to you how *I* view this, keep semantics out of the picture. In other words, it doesn't matter what you call your soul and your spirit, what matters is that you understand the concept. Furthermore, the religion you practice, or whether or not you are religious at all, does not matter here. Remember, there is but one truth. You may call your soul or spirit anything you like; the key is to realize that you have them.

Throughout this work I will refer to the spirit in a variety of ways—supreme power, innate intelligence, divine energy force, universal intelligence, etc. We will build on the concept that there is a supreme power, as discussed earlier. It is the ultimate, divine, omnipotent power; the deep, innate energy of eternity; the creator of all. This creator invented the organisms and microorganisms and all the relationships between them. It created you from two cells, a sperm and an egg. (Before you, it created the sperm and the egg. Before them, it created your parents. Before them, it created your grandparents. Way back when, it created Adam and Eve. And, even before that, it created the heavens and the earth.) This supreme power is the innate intelligence that created and runs the entire universe. This intelligence is celestial, supreme, all-knowing, and all-encompassing; it doesn't think, judge, or reason. It doesn't have to, because it is perfect.

This supreme power runs your body, just like it created your body, without the need or use of your conscious mind. This innate (inborn) intelligence is responsible for all of your internal functions. You don't have to think about your calcium level, the amount of potassium in your blood, and so on. It regulates your heart beat, your oxygen level, and keeps your fingernails growing. It keeps your cells fed and cleans up after them. Its job, within you, is survival. It does its job by responding perfectly to internal messages that zip around inside your body constantly.

It doesn't have to think or judge in order to perform the tasks of running your body. Think of this intelligence as your *sub*conscious mind. It is there inside of you, running your body, helping you to survive, without the aid of your conscious mind. This perfect, innate intelligence is what I call your spirit.

Webster defines spirit as: "1. That which is traditionally believed to be the vital principle or animating force within living beings 2. The Holy Ghost 3. God." Your innate, *sub*conscious, spirit intelligence is perfection personified. Understand, it *never* makes a mistake—it is perfect, all the time. It was fully developed at your birth, and even before your birth, as it has been all the way back to the beginning of creation. I repeat, *this spirit lives within you*—it never leaves you. It's there within you right now, as you read this book. When you cut your finger, it heals it. When you break your leg, it mends it. It is constant and steady, never deviating from its course.

## SOUL PRINCIPLE

*It isn't until you come to a spiritual understanding of who you are—not necessarily a religious feeling, but deep down, the spirit within—that you can begin to take control.*
—Oprah Winfrey

An analogy you might relate to is the computer and its programs. Think of the spirit as the master program. It is there, inside the computer. When you enter data, the computer processes it according to the program. The program runs the computer. The spirit is your program. It runs *you* according to the master program—innate intelligence or supreme power. That program, like the computer program, is constant, non-changing. It just *is*.

I often use another analogy to explain my concept of the spirit. Think of the spirit—truth, innate intelligence, supreme power, or the like—as a laser beam. It is a constant, steady, unchanging, intense beam of light. It shoots out perfectly straight, no matter what. You can run through it, cross from one side to the other, dart back and forth across it, jump into and out of its path, but it never moves. It stays right there, shooting straight, unswerving, never changing its course; your movement has no affect on the laser. That is how I see the spirit. It is a constant, steady stream of power. You and your actions do not affect the spirit. It is a path, so to speak. Our goal in life is to walk down that path in perfect alignment with the spirit.

Let me repeat, *the spirit is a path*—a straight, unswerving line. It doesn't change. It's intensely perfect, constant way isn't affected by what you think with your conscious mind or how you act or react. Our thoughts, emotions, feelings, attitudes, and actions do not effect this path one bit. In fact, they may lead us away from the path. Think about it like this: At birth, we are perfect. The supreme power uses the genes and information in our pool to create us. We are the perfect expression of the materials available to its grand plan to create us. So, we are actually born *on* the path of the divine, innate intelligence, the path of the supreme power and creator of all.

As we grow, we develop our conscious minds and begin to think; we either stay on this divine path or deviate from it. If we stay on the subconscious spiritual path we will reach the goals of good health, happiness, and success. However, these goals may *only* be reached by walking in harmony with this path. If or when we deviate from the perfect spiritual path, we create our own paths. I believe that any way other than the supreme being's way leads to *some degree* of ill-health, unhappiness, loneliness, discomfort, or the like. Our conscious mind determines the path we follow. (Remember, the spirit is our *sub*conscious mind.) It's time now for a more in-depth look at the conscious mind.

## SOUL PRINCIPLE

*The human mind is our fundamental resource.*
—John Fitzgerald Kennedy

On the train of thought that the spirit is the subconscious mind, let me state that your *conscious mind creates your soul.* I repeat, your conscious mind creates your soul. Your soul is a very complex compilation of energy that is unique to you. Your soul is your expression of how you use your conscious mind. Webster defines soul as: "The animating and vital principle in man credited with the faculties of thought, action, and emotion and conceived as forming an immaterial entity distinguished from but temporally coexistent with his body." It is your expression of you. Our supreme being gave us a conscious mind and enabled us to express free will—to think and reason, and to create our own souls. We each have the ability to make choices and those choices cause us to deviate from the spiritual path or radiate in harmony with it.

To further our thoughts on the conscious mind, let's go back to the computer analogy. When you first got your computer it was basically empty—no data. Sure, it had some software in there somewhere and that software was programmed to function in a certain manner (like your subconscious mind functions according to the master program). Think of your computer's software like your capability to learn and store information or data. You begin, as an infant, with software in place, ready to be used. As you experience life, you gather good and bad information and store it in your conscious mind—your computer. Like in your computer, that good and bad information is retained. Good data keeps us in alignment with the master program; bad data interferes with it.

You might not always be able to recall all of the stored information, but it is there. You just have to know how to access it. Just as a computer whiz can get inside the computer and bring up information that someone thought had been deleted by knowing which buttons to push, we, too, have the ability to recall stored information from our conscious mind. So, our conscious mind is like a computer—receiving, storing, and processing information—and so much more.

You are probably thinking, "But I'm not just a computer. I am not an inanimate object. I have feelings and consciousness." You are so right, we are very different from a computer in this manner. We do have feelings, beliefs, and emotions. We can think, judge, and reason: this is the "human" side of us. This, too, is our soul—this part of us that has feelings, is emotional, and forms beliefs and attitudes. And keep in mind, all of these beliefs, emotions, feelings, and attitudes are stored in our computer, whether good or bad. We are therefore a very complex, *living* computer. We have already established that the spirit is the ultimate master program. On that note, the goal in life is to get our computers (or souls) compatible with the supreme program (or spirit). This compatibility was intended by your supreme power, and will allow for your happiness, good health, and success.

Your soul and spirit combine to create the energy fields of your body. Remember the analogy of the spirit being a path—a straight, unchanging, unswerving path. To take that analogy one step further, when your soul is on the same path as your spirit, health is an automatic result. *The ultimate goal is to become as one in soul and spirit.*

## Fields of Health

**Everything that is alive pulsates with energy and all of this energy contains information.**
—Caroline Myss, Ph.D.

What do I mean by energy fields? I mean the same energy fields that scientific devices have recorded surrounding the body. The energy fields that surround your body are chaotic, all-inclusive energy. In this case, chaotic is good. A chaotic field is actually complete; it contains all the energy information available. Your personal energy field that surrounds your body is an integral part of your physical body. So, what is in your energy field has a direct impact on your health. Every energy field contains information. If your field is full of negative energy and information, then your body and your health are adversely influenced. The result may be discomfort, pain, disease, and the like. If your field is radiating with positive energy and information, then your body and health are enhanced. You feel good and are healthy.

You may be thinking, "What makes the energy in my field positive or negative? Where does the field come from? What is the field made of? Do I have any control over my field? Is it there all the time? How does this field affect me? Will it hurt me?" I believe the energy field of the body is the most vital, contributing factor in the determination of your health. To fully appreciate how internal and external energy fields relate to health, it is helpful to develop a clear picture of where we, as individuals, came from. It is not my intention to enter into the creation and evolution controversy, nor to present a treatise on sex education. However, an unbreakable link connects our understanding of health with our understanding of how the human body develops.

Much has been written about recent developments in research concerning the affect of electrical fields on physiological development of embryos. Currents emanating from an embryo are measurable outside the embryo. Evidence of electrical influence in this development is mounting. Many studies have been done to assess the presence and effects of electrical currents, ranging from studies of primitive beings, such as algal eggs and newts, to research on higher forms of life. These studies have confirmed the presence of currents during embryonic development. Researchers Lionel Jaffe and Claudio Stern report, "Recent explorations with a vibrating probe show that a wide variety of developing systems drive strong steady electrical currents through themselves ... substantial evidence indicates that these currents—or at least some of them—act back to affect development."[1] The researchers measured voltage above the primitive streak (which exists in the initial phase of development) of chick embryos and found that "steady currents with exit densities of the order of 100 microamperes per square centimeter leave the whole streak and return elsewhere through the epiblast."[2] Sounds heavy! What does this mean? It simply means that electrical current flows from inside the embryo to just outside the embryo, then returns.

# SOUL PRINCIPLE

*Biological sciences will in the end take the lead, for without life, there is no science.*

—Jacques Cousteau

Findings of a direct electrical connection between the interior and exterior of the embryo during development support my concepts that there is a direct connection and continuous energy communication between internal and external fields. Jaffe and Stern are among the many researchers who support these findings.

There is an energy field around the very first cell of every living organism. When that cell duplicates, the energy around the cell duplicates to encompass the second cell, and so it goes with the third cell and every cell thereafter. Every cell of your body is encapsulated with this energy field and, ultimately, your entire body is full of this energy field. The energy field actually radiates within and all around your physical body. This energy field contains the innate energy and information that holds the master program. It is the supreme power, the divine intellect, the spirit, or whatever you want to call it. Many different names have been given to this energy field over the years by different groups of people. It has been referred to as prana, chi, life force, odic force, aura, and innate intelligence. I like to think of this energy or intelligence as your spirit. It is the spiritual intelligence.

I believe that only by accepting the major role of energy fields as determinants of growth and health will scientists find answers to questions such as: How do cells know what they are supposed to do? How do wounds heal? What turns off the healing process? How do arms grow to the right proportional length? Why do they stop growing?

For example, it is accepted that bone-length growth is governed by estrogen. Understanding why or how estrogen or other development-regulating hormones are produced is less clear, but I believe this is paramount to understanding the innate wisdom of the body. The spiritual (innate, supreme) energy and its communication within the body is the key. Something exterior to the embryo precipitates the embryo's formation and the rhythmic pulsations.

The question remains: what or where is the organizing "command post" that directs the development of an embryo as a part of the grand design or master program? It isn't a voluntary activity in the mind of the mother. Ordinarily, several weeks of development have passed before the mother is even aware that she is pregnant. The mother isn't in charge of the schedule of development. The fetus certainly isn't in charge. According to researchers, including Jan Langman, M.D., author of *Medical Embryology: Human Development—Normal and Abnormal,* the fetus is into the second week of development before the primitive streak (the precursor to the nervous system) even begins to appear.

## SOUL PRINCIPLE

*The subtle energetic fields precede and organize the formation of the physical form as a vehicle of expression for higher conscious energies.*

—Richard Gerber, M.D.

There is no conscious direction on the part of any person that guides the pattern of development of a growing fetus. Yet every facet of the "production schedule" is carried out on time and in the proper sequence. An intelligence of some sort directs the activity of the genes of DNA, suppressing some and activating others. Since conscious thought is not involved, it is logical to infer that the motivation comes from another source. Again, I believe that source is the ultimate, spiritual energy field—the supreme intelligence that created and runs the entire universe according to its grand design or master program.

Science has shown that this energy field exists and that it influences living systems. The question of degree of influence on human health will be widely debated and researched in the twenty-first century as public pressure demands a return to a holistic view of the body. In my opinion, this will allow for a more effective and complete form of health care. I believe that health care has come full-circle since the beginning of recorded time. I was recently sent a clever depiction of this. I am uncertain of the author, but it is called "A Short History of Medicine." It goes like this:

"Doctor, I have an earache."
500 B.C. —"Here, eat this root."
300 A.D. —"That root is heathen. Say this prayer."
1750 A.D. —"That prayer is superstition. Drink this potion."
1900 A.D. —"That potion is snake oil. Swallow this pill."
1945 A.D. —"That pill is ineffective. Take this antibiotic."
2000 A.D. —"That antibiotic is artificial. Here, eat this root."

This oversimplifies my point, but you get the picture. People today question what is best for their health. Awareness that medicine does not hold all the answers is in the forefront of curing chronic diseases. More and more people are returning to a holistic, natural approach to health. People are taking charge of their health, and therefore their lives. The answers were always there, we are just finding them again

The human body is a more complete entity than casual observation would suggest. Around every living system is an energy field which is an integral part of that system. Not only does each entity possess its own field, but each component of that entity (cells, tissues, organs, and the atoms and electrons that make up those components) is encapsulated in its own field. Furthermore, adjacent fields blend to influence one another, thereby creating another field. Because electrons, protons, atoms, molecules, and all other apparently distinct structures are moving and coming in contact with other structures, the energy field of one constantly contacts and interacts with the energy field of another. Consequently, the energy fields of any living being are in a constant state of change. The human body, therefore, might be described as a teeming mass of energy. This energy field is a combination of spiritual energy and the energy of the soul. It is the spiritual or divine energy and knowledge that is behind all creation. This spiritual energy or field has the primary role in the creation, maintenance, and operation of your physical body.

Your  spiritual energy field (subconscious mind) and your soul energy field (conscious mind/physical body) influence one another, which means that maximum healing is possible only when the fields that you are made of are in tune with one another. You must resonate harmoniously with the fields of the universe. My concepts in this arena are also held by others who advocate this vitalistic principle of all-encompassing holistic healing. Gabriel Cousens, M.D. wrote in his introduction to *Vibrational Medicine: New Choices for Healing Ourselves*, by Richard Gerber, M.D.: "We, as human organisms, are a series of interacting multidimensional subtle-energy systems, and that if these energy systems become imbalanced there may be resulting pathological symptoms which manifest on the physical/emotional/mental/spiritual planes."[3] This means that if our soul energy is not in balance with the spiritual energy, then we may experience disease or ill health on the physical/emotional/mental/spiritual plane. Dr. Cousens is the author of *Spiritual Nutrition and the Rainbow Diet*.

Our soul energy field is our vital communication link between us and the spiritual energy field. The information communicated between these fields is the primary determinant of health. We either resonate with and are in harmony with the ultimate, spiritual energy source, or we are out of sync with that source. Balance and harmony with the spiritual energy results in good health, physically and mentally; disharmony with the spirit results in ill-health, discomfort, or disease. So, can this energy be utilized in the health care profession? And, more importantly, how do we harvest the energy of our field to become in balance with the spiritual energy?

# Harvesting the Energy of the Fields

We have established the concept of fields around the earth and around matter that moves with the earth, like living organisms. *Encyclopedia Britannica* has this to say about electromagnetic fields: "Around every particle, whether it be at rest or in motion, whether it be charged or uncharged, there are potential fields of various kinds." The following are a few of the many individuals who have performed intensive research and study on electric and magnetic energy fields: Kyoichi Nakagawa, M.D.; Robert Becker, M.D.; Deepak Chopra, M.D.; Gary Selden; Harold Saxton Burr, Ph.D.; Richard Gerber, M.D.; Arthur Guyton, M.D.; W. Brugh Joy, M.D.; Valerie Hunt; Stanley Krippner; Daniel Rubin; George Leonard; Bjorn Nordentrom, M.D.; Karagulla Shafica, M.D.; Cyril Smith; Simon Best; T. M. Srinivasan; William Tiller, Ph.D.; Peter Tompkins; Christopher Bird; Aubrey Westlake; Caroline Myss, Ph.D.; Candace Pert, and the list goes on and on. As you can see, I am not alone in my postulates of the energy field concept. In fact, the number of scientists, doctors, and healers who are authoring books on the subjects is growing daily.

You might be wondering, "What is it that makes Dr. Morter unique?" I see my uniqueness in the fact that I can turn you on to your own powers, so that you may help yourself to a healthier, happier, and more successful life. Another unique characteristic of mine is the fact that I have developed a healthcare technique that addresses the energy fields of the body and the relationship between these fields and the thoughts and emotions of the mind. The fact that I believe that you have more to do with your health than you may realize and the fact that I want to enlighten you by this truth have led me to write this book. It is my goal to share with you the concepts of the energy fields of your soul and your spirit; to show you how you can harvest the energies of these fields, and to reap the rewards to create optimum health. Or, conversely, to show you that you can interfere with your spiritual energy and create disease, discomfort, or distress. It's your choice. It's "soully" up to you.

## SOUL PRINCIPLE

*What you believe, you create in your field, and you will become.*

—Dr. M.T. Morter, Jr.

Japanese researcher, Kyoichi Nakagawa, M.D., cites a variety of symptoms that can be attributed to disharmony in the energy fields surrounding the body, ranging from stiff muscles to chronic constipation to headaches to "general lassitude." "In other words," writes Nakagawa, "it is a syndrome in which no objective pathological findings can be noticed from routine and clinical examinations, but in which the subjective symptoms persist and are hard to improve. ... an unbalanced nervous system or part of such might be included in this syndrome."[4] Nakagawa's conclusion that less energy reaches the body in pathological conditions coincides with my premise that interference in energy flow is the primary cause of disease.

Again, with time and experience, I have come to understand that the electromagnetic fields surrounding every living system are the focal point of health. Good health can be described as the body (or any other living system) functioning in symmetry and balance with its visible and invisible energy fields.

You may have heard, read about, or experienced auras. Auras are a combination of soul and spiritual energy fields surrounding living systems. These same fields are measured with Kirlian photography. Dr. Valerie Hunt presents a major discovery of the human field "chaos" pattern in her book, *Infinite Mind*. Her findings lead to more information about the mind and body, the emotions and creativity, "extrasensory human capacities in higher consciousness, and the mystical connections of spirit." She is credited for being the first to "discover vibration patterns during pain, disease and illness, and in emotional and spiritual states" and ... she "has found scientific evidence of individualized field signatures and subtle energetic happenings between people and within groups."[5]

Medical science is now using electromagnetic energy fields for both diagnoses and therapy. Magnetic resonance imaging (MRI) is one of the better known and currently accepted diagnostic techniques. Magnetic fields are also being used therapeutically in such areas as "field-induced hyperthermia" and a "method for magnetically removing leukemic cells from bone marrow ... to successfully treat a child with common acute lymphocytic leukemia." The electrical energy created by the brain is recorded by an electroencephalogram (EEG). The nerve activities that cause muscles to shorten (thereby stimulating the lungs, heart, blood vessels, and such) create electrical currents which are recorded by an electromyogram (EMG). And, of course, the electrocardiogram (EKG) records electrical heart activity.

As investigations continue, research into healing properties of electromagnetic fields leads to various conclusions. The bottom line is that medical science has not only identified the existence of these energy fields, it is harvesting the energy from the field and using it to diagnose, as well as treat, patients. I'm telling you that you, too, can harvest this energy and reap the reward of good health. The Booster Thoughts, or daily lessons, in Part II will give you many practical methods and examples of this power within you.

# Internal Space

Here's a quick science lesson, not intended to oversimplify or insult your existing knowledge of the material presented. Science has proven, observed, and measured these concepts.

Basically, the body is made up of matter. Matter consists of atoms, molecules, and electrons. Electrons move, which implies space for movement to take place. Electrons spin and orbit the nucleus in the unrestricted space of an atom. In other words, there is unoccupied space inside of the tiny, microscopic atom.

## SOUL PRINCIPLE

*Subatomic particles are separated by huge gaps, making every atom more than 99.999 percent empty space.*
—Deepak Chopra, M.D.

Now that's a lot of empty space! I believe that, with the ever-developing field of science, our generally accepted perception of this empty space may change. However, as we know now, there is space within the body that is not necessarily a part of the physical body, but which does contain information.

Consider the structure of cytoplasm. Prior to the development of the electron microscope, the cytoplasm of cells was understood to be a jelly-like mass that merely surrounded organelles and filled apparently unoccupied areas of the cell. When ultra high-powered instruments became available, the mass that had been thought of as nondescript was seen to contain a vast network of minute interconnecting canals of the endoplasmic reticulum. In other words, it was not just a "jelly-like mass." It had a structure and a purpose.

Areas that today are considered "empty space" may, in the future, be found to contain substances which currently are unidentified, yet which perform a distinct function. I believe that function may be intercellular communication or the relay of "spirit" information. The information that comes from the supreme intelligence (that spiritual energy that created us and the rest of the universe), the same energy or intelligence that is responsible for the master program. This empty space within the body, in which electrons orbit and move, make up the medium which harbors and transmits innate information throughout the body. In the late eighteenth century, an Austrian physician named Franz Mesmer proclaimed an existence of a "subtle fluid which pervades the universe, and associates all things in mutual intercourse and harmony."[6] Maybe soon science can prove this maxim of universal energy and communication that has been believed to be true for centuries.

The transmitted information referred to here is not that which is received through the sensory system and processed by the central nervous system. Innate information, available to the body through intra-body space, is more fundamental to life than is sensory information. Sensory information concerns present-time conditions: you get cold, so you put on a jacket. Innate, spiritual information concerns universal conditions unhampered by time. This information alters the physiological system which, in turn, sends altered signals back to influence the spiritual information. In other words, this information regulates your heartbeat, determines your calcium level, maintains adequate oxygen supply throughout your bloodstream, controls your insulin level, and so on. It is a perpetual interchange of energy.

As I said earlier, characteristics of spiritual information (or spiritual energy) and sensory information or soul energy constantly influence each other, and therefore constantly change each other. Furthermore, *if your sensory information—your soul energy field—resonates harmoniously with innate information — your spiritual energy field—then good health is the result.* When you use your conscious mind to disrupt the natural flow of spiritual energy, you interfere with the master program. Christians believe Adam and Eve were the first to interfere with the master plan. They performed the "original interference" when they chose to go against God's plan and eat the apple to satisfy their desire of taste.

In summary, empty space within us is filled with spiritual intelligence. It is this innate, spiritual intelligence that created the heavens and the earth and all living things. This intelligence takes an acorn and turns it into a mighty oak; it takes one human cell and creates a beautiful human being. This same intelligence is within us, has always been and will always be with us, surrounding us. This internal or empty space is the innate spiritual intelligence that holds our communication link with the master program.

The energy fields of your soul and spirit actually determine your level of health. It is time to consider what you can and should do to maintain or improve your current state of health. What choices do you have? How does your conscious mind *really* affect your health? Read on to understand the importance of your decisions and how the decisions you make in six essential areas affect and determine your health.

# CHAPTER 2

# YOUR MIND MATTERS

**Our minds have unbelievable power over our bodies.**

—Andre Maurois

God gave us the ability to use our conscious minds freely—free will. We use our conscious minds to make decisions and choices. We all have choices, many choices, how you choose to use your mind is up to you The choices you make in the six main areas of your life establish your level of health, resulting in good health or poor health. You may be pain-free or pain-riddled. You may be at ease or diseased. You may be symptom-free, but out of energy. Whatever your state of health is, it is a direct result of the choices you have made to this point in time in these six areas. The Six Essentials for Life are:

What you eat
What you drink
How you exercise
How you rest
What you breathe
What you think

At this point you may be thinking that these are really six essentials for health. Again, that's semantics. The point is that this is a really beautiful part of the master plan. God gave us free will. He didn't tell us what to think or how to choose, but gave us the ability to do so freely. In addition, your life and your health are directly affected by the choices you make in these six areas. So essentially, your health is your choice.

Furthermore, your lifestyle is the combination of your choices. Your soul is an expression of your conscious choices, therefore *you* are an expression of your conscious choices. It is not my intention to place blame or guilt on anyone for their state of health. I merely see and understand these six principles to be factual. I did not make the rules, but I intend to explain them as I know them to be. Let's briefly address each of the six areas and how your choices might affect your health, physically or mentally.

# The Six Essentials for Life

Life, we learn too late, is in the living, in the tissue of each day and hour.
—Stephen Butler Leacock

**WHAT YOU EAT**

I feel certain that the vast majority of you will agree that what you eat and drink has an impact on your health. Unless you have been hiding under a rock most of your life, you have read or heard on television that your diet affects your health. A steady barrage of junk food and soda pop will most likely result in illness of some kind. We all know about the four food groups, or more recently, the food pyramid. We know we need to eat a well-balanced diet, choosing from each food group or level of the pyramid and we know that certain percentages of our diet should come from each of these areas. We need to eat more fruits and vegetables, less sugar and salt. I believe, due to my many years of practice as a healthcare professional, that the amount of dietary animal protein should be greatly reduced from the commonly recommended level. (My clinical experience has proven that too much protein, from an animal source, can lead to discomfort and disease. Animal protein has an acidifying effect on the body, which is contrary to healthy functioning of the body.) These are standards that we're all aware of to some degree.

Here's a little lesson in body chemistry. You may recall the pH scale from your junior high school science class. If not, as a refresher, the pH scale is highly alkaline on one end and highly acidic on the other. For optimum health, the pH level of the body should be closer to the alkaline side. You might be able to relate to the pH of a swimming pool. When the water of a swimming pool has the right pH, it is clear and beautiful. This is much like the body. Your body requires a certain pH to function optimally. The body is *alkaline by design and acid by function*. By this I mean that your cells work best in a slightly alkaline environment, but these same cells produce acid as they work. Foods that have an alkalizing effect on the body include fruits and vegetables. That's why people who eat lots of veggies generally seem to be healthier than those who don't.

I believe that the reason veggie eaters seem to be healthier is that their bodies aren't in damage-control mode trying to subdue excess dietary acid. You see, most vegetables and fruits don't leave hard-to-eliminate acid. On the contrary, most fruits and vegetables leave ingredients that actually help the body neutralize hard-to-eliminate acid; they help to keep your body alkaline and your cells work best in that internal environment. We are talking in ideals here. Remember, the goal of eating is to sustain life.

## SOUL PRINCIPLE

*One should eat to live, not live to eat.*

—Benjamin Franklin

Now, back to the fact that working cells produce acid. The truth is, just about everything you do causes your cells to generate internal acid. Eating, breathing, playing golf, scratching your elbow, flicking the TV remote, sumo wrestling. Even thinking! So your body produces acid all the time. It's a standard body response. Hold it! I can see the question marks glistening in your eyes as you think, "You were saying acid is not a good thing and that your subconscious mind is always perfect. Yet, now you say it produces acid." Well, acid production by your body in response to physical events *is* perfect; this self-produced acid can be easily eliminated. However, the acid residue of food is a different story.

There's a big difference between the acid your body produces and the acid leftovers of your lunchtime hamburger. Self-made acid is weak, hamburger acid is relatively strong. That's the first difference. The second difference is that getting rid of weak self-made acid is a breeze. You get rid of it when you breathe. Part of what you exhale is the remnants of acid your body generates. Hamburger (and other animal protein) acid is too strong to go out through your lungs. Strong acid travels through your digestive tract to get out of your body. Much of it is processed through the kidneys and eliminated in your urine. That's why your urine can give you clues to the acid level of your internal environment. The urine, as well as saliva, can be tested with simple pH tests.

Foods that have an acidifying effect on the body include (but are not limited to): beef, chicken, pork, fish, bread, beer, chocolate cake, cheese, doughnuts, eggs, peanuts, and white rice. A more thorough list is provided in Part II, "Thoughts on What You Eat and Drink." I actually believe what you eat, on the average, five days per week, every week, establishes your health. In order to maintain good health, you must retain a certain level of alkaline reserve in your body. Your alkaline reserve is your body's store of alkalinity. The alkaline reserve serves to neutralize acid in the body. When that level of alkalinity is depleted through the process of neutralizing acidifying foods, you will experience pangs of ill-health. Although symptoms vary from individual to individual, you will move from a sense of being at ease to a sense of disease.

In summary, what you eat is your choice. Poor choices lead to ill health or disease, while good choices lead to improved energy and vitality. There is no substitute for a good diet, rich in nature's bounty of fruits and vegetables. Whole foods, grown in rich soil, provide the exact ratio of vitamins, nutrients, and minerals essential for a well-balanced diet, which leads to a healthy body.

The key here is *whole foods*, not *parts of foods*, and rich soil. Herbicides and pesticides are man-made chemicals that may keep the pests away, but they are also harmful to the internal flora of the human body. Organically grown foods are far superior, but not always easy to get. Genetically engineered food may prove to be the greatest harm to good nutrition since the beginning of time. Plants and animals have evolved, naturally, over the course of millions of years. As certain species deviated or changed in their development, they perished. They simply no longer fit into the synergy of the remainder of living things. They could not find the nutrients they now needed to survive or reproduce. If a plant changed in this manner and perished, then the animals that fed upon that plant perished, too. This is nature, a part of the grand plan. The problem with genetically engineered food is that it is man-made; it is not natural. We have no long-term studies to reveal its effects on the ecosystem as a whole. This food may serve to wipe out animal species or other plant life. The majority of the soy beans planted this year are genetically engineered, yet this strain of soy bean has only been in existence for about five years. Five years—and now part of an ecosystem that has been evolving for millions of years! This is cause for great concern, as it is impossible for man to improve on nature. It may take years to realize and understand the ultimate outcome of genetically engineered food.

As a result of depleted soil, herbicides, pesticides, and genetically engineered foods, it may be necessary to supplement the diet with natural food supplements or minerals. Natural food supplements, vitamins, herbs, and minerals—in the proper proportion for you—may aid in increasing your alkaline level, thus improving your overall health. Choosing the right supplements is very important. Look for food supplements, vitamins, or minerals that are all-natural and not heat-processed, as heat destroys the molecular structure and denatures the protein.

**WHAT YOU DRINK**

You can survive for weeks without food, but only for a matter of days without water. Cells function in a fluid environment. Without adequate fluids, cells can't function. Since the body is over one-half water, it stands to reason that water is vital to your body. Fluid replacement is essential to life, but any time fluid (or any other substance) is put into the body, the body is stressed—

it must change the way it is functioning to process the new substance. Even water must be processed, although it causes the least internal upheaval. It should come as no surprise that drinking even common, everyday drinks—such as coffee, tea, cola, and alcoholic beverages—puts greater stress on the body than does drinking pure water. The body must not only process the drinks, it must also contend with their stimulating effects. Problems can arise when stimulants are an integral part of your regular diet. Unremitting stimulation, whether from worry and anxiety or from coffee and alcohol, is unremitting stress.

As a practical matter, we all get thirsty. The fluids lost through elimination, perspiration, and breathing must be replenished. What are some good drink choices? The most healthful beverages you can drink to satisfy your thirst are pure water and juices made from fresh fruits and/or vegetables. I recommend water purified by the reverse osmosis method. Distilled water is the next best alternative. There is no substitute for pure water. It is *vital* to a healthy existence.

## SOUL PRINCIPLE

*Water is the only drink for a wise man.*
—Henry David Thoreau

### HOW YOU EXERCISE

This topic has shared the limelight with diet over the past few years. You can hardly pick up the newspaper or flip through channels on the TV without coming across something about exercise. It seems every fitness expert has his or her own exercise regime or equipment to enhance the physical body—everything from one-hour aerobic workouts, to videos and equipment concentrating on specific body parts. Exercise programs run the gamut from running five miles per day to choosing to use the stairs instead of the escalator. Any or all of these exercise programs might be right for you. It is very important to find out what *is* right for you.

Keeping the body agile, strong, and hardy is paramount to overall good health. You need exercise. No matter what your physical condition, you need to move those parts that will move. Properly executed exercise benefits both young and mature bodies. At any age, men and women who exercise regularly enjoy increased mobility and muscle tone, improved cardiovascular function, and improved balance. Yet, exercise doesn't guarantee good health. While exercise is necessary, it is still only one factor in the determination of good health.

Many Americans are virtually obsessed with trying to be healthy and fit. Jogging, aerobics, stair-climbing, spinning, racquetball, walking, swimming, weight-lifting—you name it, Americans are panting to be sleek, in shape, and fit. One indicator of our passion for perspiration is the number of TV ads touting various types of exercise equipment and keep-in-shape videos. Although few of us will ever look like the perfect-body role models featured on TV and in magazines, thousands of people stretch, bend, high-step, and bounce rhythmically and regularly in an attempt to reach that impossible dream.

In order for any exercise program to be truly effective in improving your health, it must be a whole-body exercise, one that integrates and balances the body. Your exercise program should do *all* of the following:

1. improve joint articulation, muscle tone, and resiliency ("grease the knees" and loosen up the muscles),
2. enhance cardiovascular efficiency (tune up your heart and tone up your blood vessels),
3. contribute to physio-neurological integration (improve body–mind balance), and
4. improve timing signals to opposing muscles (remove "internal static").

Since your body is a unified structure, everything affects everything else. To reap the greatest benefits of exercise, you need to work your whole body as a unit. This means you should be sure to involve those areas of your body that aren't involved in your everyday activities. Involve those muscles you only know exist after shoveling snow or romping through a tag football game at the company picnic. It is important to note here that exercising certain muscle groups in order to "body-build," like you are training for the Mr. Universe physique, is quite different than whole-body exercise. It's okay to focus on increasing muscle mass of particular muscle groups, if that's your goal. Just don't confuse body-building with health-building. These are two entirely different beasts.

Before you launch a campaign of body-building or any exercise program, check with your doctor to be sure you are healthy enough to withstand the rigors of the intensified physical activity. Your doctor can make sure your heart and cardiovascular system will tolerate the increased work load for your particular exercise program.

It is important to note that the pH level of the body, which we discussed in relation to diet and nutrition, also comes into play here. You need to know if the acid level or pH level of your body is within acceptable limits—that is, on the alkaline side of neutral—since exercise produces physiologic acid. If your internal environment is in the neutral to slightly alkaline range, the additional physiologic acid is no problem. (Remember, this is the type of acid that is easily eliminated when you breathe.) However, if your body is already overly acidic, strenuous exercise can be harmful. So the controlled acid-alkaline (pH) test is essential to determine the acid level of your body before you start a rigorous exercise program.

You may have heard about the twenty-five-year-old athlete, a model example of fitness, who dropped dead during a basketball game. Or the "perfectly healthy" forty-year-old man who died of a heart attack while on his morning jog. Did this ever seem confusing to you? Did you ever wonder why these "fit" people died while exercising? I believe, based on my many years of clinical experience with thousands of patients, that the pH level of these people was too acidic. The pH test referred to earlier could have been an indicator to them that they were not ready for strenuous exercise.

Exercise should make you feel good, both physically and mentally. How you feel about the exercise you do greatly enhances or diminishes the overall benefits you derive from your efforts.

The key to a healthy exercise plan is to: first, take action; second, like what you do; and third, accomplish a goal of fitness that you desire.

## SOUL PRINCIPLE

*It is only the constant exertion and working of our sensitive, intellectual, moral, and physical machinery that keeps us from rusting, and so becoming useless.*
—Charles Simmons

I have a favorite recommendation for a whole-body exercise. It requires no special equipment, no monthly fee, no reservations, scant training, and is suitable for solitary, pair, or group participation. All you really need to get started is a conscious choice, appropriate shoes, and seasonal clothing. What is this gem of an exercise? Walking.

Walking in fresh outdoor air is the aerobic exercise choice for people of all ages. You reap all the benefits of healthful exercise during a brisk walk. Properly done, walking improves muscle tone and elasticity, tones up your cardiovascular system, and helps to fine-tune muscle movement. You should walk in a contralateral fashion. In other words, extend your right arm and left leg at the same time, then left arm and right leg. Ideally, if you are in reasonably good condition you should be able to step off a mile in about fifteen minutes—but maybe not the first time out the door.

Exercise sessions should be divided into three parts: warm-ups, work outs, and cool downs. Begin your program slowly. Stretch out your muscles before you take off. After you've warmed up and limbered out, walk as fast as is comfortable for you to get your heart rate up to about 120 beats per minute. (Wear a watch; it won't throw you off balance.) You will know if you can sustain this pace for ten or fifteen minutes. Your body will give you plenty of clues as to how it's handling the stress. If you find you are gasping for breath, or if you can feel your heart pounding, slow down or stop. After you have regained your breath and your heart beat returns to normal, continue at a more moderate speed. As long as you can talk and smile as you walk, continue. Your goal should be to walk at 120 paces per minute with your heart rate at 120 beats per minute for fifteen minutes. You can then slow down for about five additional minutes, as a cool-down.

**HOW YOU REST**

The media has also given a fair amount of attention to the importance of sleep and rest. There is a huge difference between sleep and rest. Many patients have said, "Doc, I sleep ten or eleven hours a night and I wake up just as tired as I was when I went to bed." How can this be? Simple. Thoughts and emotions rob them of healthful, restorative rest. These patients are as tense when they sleep as they are when they're awake. The master program does not require sleeping medications either. That's sleeping— but not resting.

Rest and sleep are necessary for your body to rejuvenate, recuperate, and restore. That cannot take place when you crawl into bed at night exhausted, then lie there and relive all of the frustrations, hurts, injustices, indignities, and general negativities of the day and the past. How can your body slip out of its defense mode when you constantly feed it threatening thoughts? When disturbing, anxiety-provoking thoughts run rampant through your conscious mind as you finally fall asleep, you feed those thoughts into your subconscious mind, thus forcing it to respond to defend you, for your survival. You aren't even aware that you are doing it.

I believe that falling asleep while you're in defense physiology (when you are uptight, tense, worried, frustrated, or the like) actually "saves" that physiology on your mental "hard drive." We will discuss the power of your thoughts in detail later; for now let's continue to address the importance of rest.

The first clue that something is interfering with your rest and rehabilitation is that you wake up just as tired as you were when you went to bed. Then you spend the rest of the day becoming more tired. In an effort to get more rest, you try going to bed a little earlier. The big accomplishment there is that you lie awake longer fretting and stewing about everything that went wrong that day, including the fact that you are so tired.

Lack of adequate sleep and rest can do more than make you

grouchy and petulant. Long-term sleep deprivation can have profound effects. One sleep deprivation study showed that a seventeen-year old who went eleven days without sleep exhibited "brief hallucinations and easily controlled episodes of bizarre behavior" after five to ten days. On the whole, the student experienced "irritability, blurred vision, slurring of speech, memory lapses, and confusion concerning his identity."[7] Fortunately, no long-term after effects remained.

## SOUL PRINCIPLE

*Regimen is better than physic. Every one should be his own physician. We ought to assist, and not to force nature. Eat with moderation what agrees with your constitution.*
*Nothing is good for the body but what we can digest. What medicine can procure digestion? Exercise. What will recruit strength? Sleep. What will alleviate incurable evils? Patience.*

—Voltaire

Many studies have shown that people need an average of eight hours of sleep per night. Research has shown that we can even create a "sleep debt" by not getting enough sleep for several consecutive nights. For example, if you sleep one hour less than you need each night for eight nights in a row, your brain will need sleep as desperately as if you had stayed up all night.

To control the restless sleep problem, make conscious choices. When you go to bed, exercise your freedom of choice over your thoughts and refuse to allow negativity to creep into your consciousness. Always finish your day with positive thoughts. If you must rehash the day's events, find some favorable or positive aspects of your day to think about. Be sure your evening prayer, if you say one, contains thanks for your many blessings. The main point to remember here is that your body must rest and sleep in order to rejuvenate.

## WHAT YOU BREATHE

Of the Six Essentials for Life, breathing has a distinguishing characteristic. It is the only one of the six that you can't put off for more than a few minutes without major repercussions. Breathing isn't a learned skill. You aren't plagued by trying to fit "breathing time" into an already overcrowded schedule. You don't have to go out and gather air or wait for it to go on sale. For the most part, your innate intelligence (subconscious or spirit) takes care of your breathing while you tend to other matters. It's part of the master program. Yet, despite its automatic nature, you can consciously control your breathing: you can pant, huff and puff, take in deep gulps, hyperventilate, hypoventilate, or just stop for awhile. But, under normal circumstances, if you stop for more than ten or fifteen seconds, you must concentrate on what you're doing. It doesn't take much breath-holding before you "explode" as the master program kicks in, searching for air. So, we know we must breathe, but why?

The primary purpose for breathing is to get oxygen to the cells. Cells need oxygen in order to function. They take in oxygen to use in their functioning, and as they function they produce carbon dioxide ($CO_2$). But $CO_2$ is a waste product and if the cell is full of $CO_2$, there is not enough room for new oxygen. So the $CO_2$ must be eliminated. Red blood cells carry oxygen from your lungs to other parts of your body. They also take the $CO_2$ waste back to the lungs to be eliminated. The purpose of breathing, then, is not only to bring oxygen into your body but also to get rid of waste $CO_2$. So, the master plan determined that we *will* breathe, and that breathing is an essential housekeeping activity.

But, what are the choices involved with breathing? Quality of air! Clean, fresh air is at a premium in our technological, energy-hungry world. The air we breathe is saturated with particles of man-made chemicals that get into our bodies. Fuels, noxious emissions, pesticides, chemical fertilizers, and other impurities infest our breathing material in cities, rural areas, factories, processing plants, businesses, and homes. Chemical-laden air is not healthy air to breathe. Fortunately, our bodies come equipped with marvelous cleansing and detoxifying systems that have served mankind well for thousands of years. However, these systems of your body must work overtime when you are in an environment that is chemical-intense year after year. This puts undue stress on your body.

## SOUL PRINCIPLE

*The Air Quality Act of 1967 gives the country, for the first time, a comprehensive plan for setting and enforcing standards for clean air.*

—Hervey Gilbert Machen

On the other hand, our bodies can generally handle nature's by-products without any problem at all. Nature's aromas shouldn't be toxic to your body. Scents that waft from trees, flowers, and other types of foliage titillate our senses to bring enjoyment to life. They are part of the grand scheme, the master program. You can lift your spirit and feed your soul by going for a walk in the piney woods with its natural smells and clean, fresh air.

You may be thinking, "If nature's aromas are so good, then why do I sneeze, cough, and get watery eyes when I'm in the great outdoors?" The answer to that is very simple: incorrect choices in all, or too many, of the Six Essentials for Life leave you vulnerable. There are limits to how many choice-crises the body can handle gracefully. If your body has to jump through hoops just trying to neutralize the effects of acidifying foods, lack of exercise, stress-causing drinks, contaminated air, insufficient or ineffective rest, and turbulent thoughts, the end result may be "allergies" to pollen or other natural particles that are normally non-threatening. Remember, it's the choices you make in the Six Essentials for Life that determine your total level of health. Each of these is vital to your health equation.

No discourse on breathing would be complete without a few choice words on smoking. The first word that comes to my mind regarding smoking is: DON'T. Unless you have been living in an isolated, underground, communication-free vault for the past thirty years, you are well aware of the dangers of smoking. Government agencies and health associations have waged extensive, expensive public awareness campaigns to drive home the message that smoking can kill you—or, at the very least, cause you great physical and economic pain and suffering. The perils of smoking include the increased potential for lung cancer, interference with blood circulation and the absorption/retention of some vitamins and minerals, as well as a host of other maladies. While I have never smoked beyond the few childhood trial puffs that made me sick, I believe I would have quit on the spot in college when I first viewed the black, gunk-filled "smoker's lungs" of a cadaver in anatomy dissection lab. In contrast, a non-smoker's lungs are clean and baby pink. If we wore our lungs exposed on the outside of our bodies, there would be far fewer smokers.

Respiratory toxicity from smoking or from environmental pollution imposes severe stress on the body. That stress can weaken or exhaust vulnerable organs and systems that are trying to cope with other stresses. Therefore, the additional stress of being immersed in environmental toxic waste can tip the scales to allow the development of disease. You can make conscious choices regarding the quality of air your body must contend with. If you suffer with severe respiratory allergies or respiratory disease, quality of life can be synonymous with quality of air. Radical choices and changes may be required.

But hope springs eternal. You can make the best of an unchangeable situation by making sure your choices in the other five essential areas of your life are conducive to the highest possible level of health. When you are truly healthy, your body is slightly alkaline, your soul energy field is harmonious with the spiritual energy field, and you are in the best overall condition possible to overcome negative situations.

**WHAT YOU THINK**

Now we are getting to what I believe to be the most important of the Six Essentials for Life. What you think has a greater impact on your health than the other five combined. Thoughts, or memories of thoughts, run through your head twenty-four hours a day, seven days a week—even when you sleep. You can't get away from thoughts and thoughts affect your physiology *all* of the time. Man's level of thought is what separates him from other species. I have done so much study and research on thoughts and thought processes that my colleagues have referred to me as the "thought doctor." That's okay with me. I've learned over the years, with thousands of patients, that thoughts can be creative or destructive, helpful or harmful. Thoughts are things.

The impact of thoughts on physiology can be demonstrated by this simple example. Think of a lemon. See yourself slicing that lemon in half. Now, imagine picking up one half and squeezing the juice into your open mouth. If you do this with your eyes closed and really concentrate, you can, and probably will, begin to salivate. Salivation is your body's natural response to neutralize the acid of the lemon. Just the mere thought of pure lemon juice in your mouth can change your body's physiology.

The intricate, unexplainable processes of thinking are behind all of the monumental achievements of mankind: building the pyramids; inventing the wheel; harnessing energy; creating great symphonies, works of art, literature, and architecture; developing great religions and social principles. These are just some of the steps on mankind's march of progress, including the "giant step for Mankind." Thinking is also behind the kaleidoscope of brutal horrors of man's inhumanity to man; thinking is behind most pain and misery. One of my goals in writing this book is to help you learn how your thoughts affect your health.

## SOUL PRINCIPLE

*Learning without thought is labor lost; thought without learning is perilous.*

—Confucius

Your thoughts can actually stimulate and prolong intense physiological activity. By physiological activity I mean the functions and processes of your body, its parts and organs. That's one of the key points of how my concept of the body–mind connection affects your long-term health: thoughts actually generate energy. This has been established scientifically time and again. Proven scientific devices have recorded the energy generated by the brain. It has also been established scientifically that the body is surrounded by energy which leads us to a second key point—

the connection between thoughts and health. This is a biggie. The connection between thoughts and health is the mind–field connection.

I have come to know that what you think about, you bring about. Your body responds constantly to your mind's messages. In his book, *Quantum Healing*, Dr. Chopra says, "You may not think you can talk to your DNA, but, in fact, you do continually."[8] He goes on to say that people who often think and say, "I'm sick and tired … ," shouldn't be surprised when they get sick or tired. Your verbal expressions and thoughts actually send messages to your body, which it displays in physical symptoms. In fact, specific feelings and emotions have been linked with particular symptoms and diseases. I have seen a variety of lists that make these connections, but one that you may wish to refer to is in Karol Truman's book, *Feelings Buried Alive, Never Die.*[9]

It seems that negative feelings are generally associated with the production of disease. If that is so, then the opposite postulate would be that positive feelings produce health. Proverbs 16:24 says, "Pleasant words are as an honeycomb, sweet to the soul, and health to the bones." Feeding the physical body positive thoughts from the conscious mind leads to health. Food for thought—a mind–field connection.

# Emotional Memory Override/ Subconscious Emotional Memory Override

I can't state strongly enough that your conscious mind is very powerful. You know this, yet you may not realize the full potential of your conscious mind. As I have said, God gave us the ability to think with our conscious mind—free will. Furthermore, our use of our conscious mind creates the energy field which is our soul. We use our mind to run our lives, learn, make choices, and establish beliefs and attitudes. We learn facts, figures, concepts, phone numbers, names, how to tell time, how to figure the area of a square, and how to perform various other practical and intellectual feats. We make choices like what clothes to wear, whether to smoke or not, what to eat and drink, which political candidate to support, when to rest, which book to read, when or how to exercise, and so on. Remember the analogy of the computer and the conscious mind? Our conscious mind receives, processes, and stores information like a computer. In addition, it is with our conscious minds that we develop our attitudes, beliefs, feelings, and emotions. Two key elements of the mind that we will now focus on are the abilities to store (or remember) and to feel emotions. Emotion and memory.

You've probably heard of the *fight or flight* instinct. This is a natural innate response to our environment. The fight or flight reflex produces physiology-changing responses inside our bodies for the purpose of survival. It's one of our built-in survival mechanisms and humans have come equipped with this instinct from the beginning of time. In fact, it was probably much more necessary in the days of our ancestors. For instance, when walking into a cave and meeting a bear, one's survival depended on either fighting the bear or running away. I admit that neither seems to be a great choice, but a decision had to be made right away—for survival. What happened *inside* the body of the person who met the bear is of great significance here. His body actually produced chemicals, *immediately*, to respond to the situation. Let's think about what went through this man's mind. It's fear, you say. Yes, he would have experienced immediate impact, high-voltage fear. That fear would have produced chemicals inside his body, which would have instantly changed bodily functions to allow him to respond to the situation. Among other things, his subconscious mind would have produced a great shot of adrenaline, which would have elevated his heart rate to enable him to do his best to get out of that situation. Fear was the catalyst that spurred the production of adrenaline and elevated the heart rate and it did so *instantly*. The man could have seen the bear and thought, "Oh, how cute." But, do you think he would have lived to tell about it? I don't think so. That loving thought would not have produced the adrenaline level and elevated heart rate necessary to respond in a life-saving manner. Fear actually worked in an attempt to save his life.

## SOUL PRINCIPLE

*We must face what we fear; that is the case of the core of the restoration of health.*

—Max Lerner

This story of the man and the bear is a simple dramatization of the effects of the conscious mind on the subconscious mind. A feeling of fear at the conscious level caused the immediate response of the subconscious mind to survive. But, fright doesn't have to be fear of a bear. In fact, in today's world, it most likely is not. However, we still have fear and it's just as real to us as it was to the man who found the bear in his cave. Furthermore, our bodies still respond in the same manner as bodies did back then. When you experience fear, your body responds to the chemicals automatically produced, which change your physiology in order to defend you—*defense physiology*.

Your body is programmed to handle "bears" that threaten your *physical* safety. Here's how your body was designed to work: Your conscious mind detects danger, your subconscious mind responds. In other words, the perfect, innate, spiritual intelligence responds. Physiology instantly adjusts for defense—survive or die. Either way, *the danger is over soon*. If you survive, your body goes back to normal physiology. The conscious mind receives information from the five senses, inputs information into the sensory system, and the body automatically responds to that information. That's the grand design.

Modern fears can be the fear of losing your job, getting cancer, disappointing your mother, being abused by Uncle Charlie, failing a test, or enduring loneliness. It doesn't matter what you are afraid of; what matters is the intensity and duration with which you experience your fears. In other words, if you are extremely afraid of something for a long time and you think about it often, then your body is constantly producing chemicals, thus changing systemic and organic functions in order to "fight that bear" that doesn't exist *physically*. The fear lives in your mind, not the physical level.

This causes health problems. Your body is not designed to

constantly fight bears or fears. That is too stressful and exhausting to your body and your body will express that exhaustion in
the form of illness or disease. Stress has been defined as *anything* that causes your body to change the way it is functioning.
For example, eating is a stress because your body must stop what
it was doing and digest the food. Fear is a stress. Our bodies produce chemicals and change functions in order to help us fight off
things that frighten us—all in the name of survival. However,
fright is not the only emotion that changes the way your body is
functioning. *Any* emotion prompts the body to respond in some
manner.

Recent studies continue to affirm the link between feelings
and one's state of health. For example, feeling helpless may slow
the immune system and lower the body's resistance. When under
stress, believing that you must be in control can also have an
affect on your immunity. Feeling like you should just give-up to
the stresses of your life may raise your risk of cancer or sudden
death. Extreme negative emotions like hostility, cynicism, and
distrust may play a part in your risk of heart disease and
artherosclerosis. Emotions, thoughts, beliefs, and attitudes are
not just in your mind, but are directly linked to your overall health
through electrochemical occurrences within your body—physiological responses. Roger Guillemin and Andrew Schally received
the Nobel Prize in physiology or medicine in 1977 for demonstrating that the brain uses chemical messengers to communicate with the body.

You usually know when you are stressed in a negative way.
You feel tense or irritable. When you're suddenly frightened or
startled, you can feel your body react—like when strange noises
go bump in the night, or you have to speak in front of an audi-
ence, or another car comes hurtling toward you on your side of
the road. Danger rampages and you are stressed. These are modern-day equivalents of the stress our ancestor felt when he encountered the bear in his cave.

The problem comes because thoughts and emotions you
create in your conscious mind also produce chemicals and the
body responds to the chemicals, without thought, to survive. You
fear losing your job and your body produces chemicals, which

change bodily functions in order to protect itself. As long as the chemicals are being produced, the body is going to respond to them.

You may be thinking, "Why is this a problem? I thought the subconscious innate spiritual intelligence only responds perfectly." That is true. The response by the subconscious is perfect, but the *timing* is inappropriate. In other words, when fear is a result of a life-threatening physical situation, the response of chemical production is perfect. But when the situation is not life-threatening, then the same perfect response is performed at an inappropriate time. Although it is our built-in response to the emotion according to the master program, it isn't necessary for survival at this time. Remember perfect intelligence doesn't think, judge, or reason. Therefore it doesn't think, "Okay, this fear is not really life-threatening. I think I'll just produce a little bit of adrenaline and only slightly increase the heart rate." Our bodies did not come equipped with a differentiation between physical/survival fears and fears that simply come from thoughts or memory. Your body reacts the same way to the fear of a bear as to the fear of losing your job. The same feeling is generated within you and the same chemicals are produced. It's automatic. So you go around "fighting bears" every time you fear losing your job. The subconscious instantly and perfectly responds to fear. Period.

Mental stresses, like fear of not being able to pay the bills, are different from physical stresses in another way. Mental stresses are long-lasting, not short-term. Most modern-day "bears" don't go away quickly. These bears are mortgage payments, credit card bills, impatient landlords, grumpy spouses, irritating kids, cranky bosses, and the like. You can't kill them or run away from them and you may think about them all the time. If so, you remain in a state of fear, hate, loneliness, anger, or such constantly. Then, there's no escaping it. Your body must produce chemicals to help you through the situation over and over and over again, all day long. You may wake up in the middle of the night and think about those "bears," so your body doesn't even get a chance to rest. It just keeps on pumping adrenaline and elevating your heart rate to help you survive the "bear" of the moment. Your doctor may see this as high blood pressure. I see this as defense physiology, which results from what I call *emotional memory override*. The body automatically responds to the mind's messages.

In Chapter 1, I discussed falling asleep while in defense physiology and the subsequent effects on your rest and recuperation. Defense physiology is the reaction your body has to strong negative emotions. It is a tense and stiff physiology. Defense physiology is the perfect response to feeling worried, frustrated, scared, and the like. As I stated before, falling asleep, or waking in the night, experiencing strong emotions, like fear, hate, anger, or worry, perpetuates defense physiology and actually "saves" that physiology on your mental "hard drive." As a result, later on you don't even need to think directly about the original thought (particular worry, fear, frustration, etc.) to bring it up again. All it takes to call up the whole defense physiology pattern again is to meander into a nearby thought neighborhood. Get close to the original thought with an associated thought in your mind and you hit the "restore" command for the original thought physiology of defense. This is what I call *emotional memory override*.

## SOUL PRINCIPLE

*How can such deep-imprinted images sleep in us at times, till a word, a sound, awake them?*
—Gotthold Ephraim Lessing

You are actually using your memory and emotions to override the power of the perfect spirit intelligence by forcing the program to respond to a situation that is not really life-threatening, even though the survival instinct believes it to be so. It's not part of the *intent* of the master program.

The original program allowed for responses only to physical situations, not mental ones that we create. We have evolved into beings that respond to our environment with the same emotions that our ancestors did, only the environment today is not life-threatening for most people. Not paying the bills won't kill you. The feeling of fear you experience is the same, but it is felt for too long. It is unremitting and harmful. The feeling comes from your mind or memory, not the physical world and it moves you from a state of ease to a state of *disease*, physically and/or mentally. This is physiological abuse that we lavish upon ourselves.

For a more thorough understanding of emotional memory override, let's take a little stroll down memory lane. You may be surprised to learn that memory lane is a *very* long path. Your memory lane actually goes back to the very beginning. God gave each of us a fantastic memory. It is part of the master program, the grand design, of the human being. In fact, you have a memory that is much better than you think it is. Your memory has actually stored every thought and every experience that you have ever had. The key here is that nothing is ever stored singularly, meaning, nothing is ever stored by itself. It is stored in conjunction with feelings and emotions like hate, fear, loneliness, love, or worry.

Here's how it works. You have an experience that causes you to worry. Let's say you worry and worry that you aren't going to be able to pay the rent this month. Now, if we stop to really think about this, we will all probably agree that worrying about it is not going to pay the rent, but that doesn't mean that we are all going to stop worrying. We just keep on worrying; some of us have even perfected worrying. We worry about that rent in the morning when we get up, we worry about it while we eat lunch, we worry about it some more when we go to bed at night. Worry, worry, worry. This is problem enough in itself, but the real problem is that it is not all by itself.

In fact, you have worried before, in the past. You worried that you wouldn't pass that test, that little Joey would get sick, that your mom would fall and break her hip, that Sam would have a car wreck, or something similar. The point is, the rent is not your first experience with worry. So, here's what happens. Your brain identifies that you are doing "worry" and it takes this new rent worry and stacks it neatly in the memory bank designed for worry, the "worry column." This column is actually formed in stair steps, except each step is a different size. Little worries form little steps, while big worries form giant steps. A point of interest here is that each emotion has its own stair-stepping column in your memory and every emotion produces certain chemicals that your body must respond to according to the master program in order to survive.

## Subconscious Emotional Memory Override

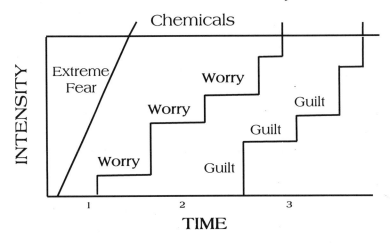

Let's say in addition to your rent worry, which formed a medium-sized stair step in your worry column, that you also have a little bitty worry you aren't going to have time to do a load of laundry before bedtime. This is not a major worry—you still have some clean clothes—but it is a nagging little worry nonetheless. This worry will also slide into the worry column, forming a little, short stair step. So, now you have added two new worries to your worry column and it is growing a bit taller. Keep in mind these two new worries have piled on top of every other worry that you have ever worried, forming a considerably tall staircase. Some of you may be thinking, "Wow, I've got the stairway to heaven for a worry column!"

The point is, every worry produces chemicals that cause your body to respond. In addition, this worry column is stacking up and stacking up, all the time. At some point, you reach a level that your body is in such a state of worry that these chemicals are produced all the time, even as you sleep. You have now reached *subconscious emotional memory override*. You don't even have to think about your rent worry or your laundry worry or any other particular worry. When you are in subconscious emotional memory override, chemicals are produced and your body must respond. This overproduction of chemicals manifests itself uniquely within each of us in the form of various ailments, symptoms, and diseases. When you worry, for example, you may get an ulcer, chronic headaches, depression, a bad cold, or lethargy. Someone else, who also worries too much, may develop high blood pressure, panic attacks, constipation, the flu, or fatigue as a result of subconscious emotional memory override.

Some of you may now be thinking, "Whew, thank goodness I'm not much of a worrier." Well, try this on for size: *every* emotion has its own stair-stepping column. That's right. Hate, fear, anger, jealousy, and every other emotion has its own column, its own storage bank in your memory. Now you may be identifying some stairways of your own. Each of those strong negative emotion produces chemicals to which the body must respond so each negative emotion can catapult you into emotional memory override.

You can also go straight to subconscious emotional memory override in one giant step. Examples that might take you directly there include: sudden death of a loved one, an automobile accident, or any sudden occurrence that impacts you dramatically on the emotional level.

One of the strongest emotions, and one that most strongly impacts human health, is fear. Our ancestors feared that bear. As children we feared the big bad wolf, the mean old man next door, or the classroom bully. Those are fears of physical objects. As adults today, we fear things like the loss of happiness, getting cancer, or losing someone we love. We fear things we don't want. We fear things we don't like. We fear things we don't know enough about. And we fear things that are not physical. A bear, a wolf, and the classroom bully are physical objects; the loss of happiness, getting cancer, and losing a loved one are not. This, again, is the key factor in emotional memory override.

In summary, if you fear over and over, you eventually live in a state of fear. Your body constantly produces the chemicals necessary to deal with your fears and responds physically to those chemicals. The fight or flight response was designed to survive physical attacks, not mental ones. The cave man felt fear of the bear, his body reacted with needed chemicals and systemic functions, and he was prepared to defend himself. Whether he actually survived or not, he fought or ran, and the whole incident was over in a matter of minutes.

Today's fears (hates, angers, worries, jealousies, etc.) are not on the physical plane and they last for a very long time. Your subconscious responds according to its master program, but the situation is not over in a matter of minutes. This continual drain of energy to fight or run exhausts your body, which manifests itself in your health. It may lead to illness, disease, pain, a bad cold, the flu, or depression. Continually exhausting your power to fight puts you on the road to poor health. Fear and other strong negative emotions are major contributors to exhausting your body.

Keep in mind that *every* emotion produces certain chemicals in your body that your body must respond to in order to survive. Dr. Blair Justice offers extensive research on how the brain and body interact in his book, *Who Gets Sick*. He cites information from leading researchers regarding chemicals, neurotransmitters, and hormones, their related bodily functions, and the outcome on the physical body when produced in excess. Neurotransmitters are, simply put, chemicals that transmit nerve impulses. These are the chemical messengers that Roger Guillemin and Andrew Schally received the Nobel Prize for demonstrating back in the 1970s during a series of important studies. I recommend *Who Gets Sick* to anyone who is interested in a more in-depth study in this area. Dr. Justice has this to say:

> "The new knowledge of how our brains profoundly affect the functioning and malfunctioning of our internal organs has far-ranging implications for our health. Of key importance is the way the brain and body use a variety of chemical messengers to carry on proper communication among our 100 trillion cells.
>
> The discovery that our very attitudes, beliefs and moods influence the action of the messengers has greatly expanded knowledge of how we can get sick— or, conversely, protect our health. For instance, when we are chronically hostile, excessive secretion of one of these neurochemicals—norepinephrine—contributes to our risk of hypertension, arteriosclerosis or a heart attack. When we believe our problems are be-

yond control, another hormone—cortisol—increases and can impair our immune system, making us more vulnerable to infections and some cancer. When we think we cannot cope effectively, still another chemical messenger—dopamine, which is related to our sense of reward and pleasure—diminishes. On the other hand, when we have a sense of being able to cope, when we have a sense of control or self-efficacy, our stress hormones—cortisol, norepinephrine, and epinephrine—decline."[10]

In addition to the fact that emotions evoke chemical production and bodily response, *you can also never forget anything.* If a memory causes you discomfort, then you must learn to be able to recall it, and process your feelings about it differently.

Keep in mind that your reaction to life's stresses play a major role in your health. Just because you don't worry doesn't mean you're off the hook. You may live in fear, or guilt, or in a world of loneliness, judgment, or indecision. All emotions produce chemicals. The crux of the matter is that at some point your body is weakened by this constant "bear fight" and you go into subconscious emotional memory override. You may get neck strain, back pain, a cold, the flu, cancer, depression, arthritis, gall stones, or an infection. It doesn't matter what you "get," what does matter is that you recognize *why* you got it. I believe you actually "earn" it, with your unremitting chain of thoughts and emotions. When physical or mental symptoms appear, most people run to the medical doctor to get a special pill or potion—a "fix." In my opinion, pills and potions simply mask the symptoms. They don't treat the cause, they treat the *effect* of the cause.

When you use your memory and emotions to override the program of innate intelligence, you create disharmony between your energy fields. You actually create disease, discomfort, depression, or ill health of some nature. Disharmony leads you away from the spiritual path. In Part II, Booster Thoughts, there are many lessons to help you conquer your thoughts and emotions and allow harmony in your life.

It is my insatiable search for this harmony and the truth in how the body, mind, and spirit work together to create our over-all state of being that has led me through the past four decades. I have stated that I do not profess to be an historical scholar of the Bible. In fact, I am continually studying biblical works, Chris-tianity, and other religions to further my knowledge in this area. On the other hand, I am not such a scientist that I believe that science has all the answers either. I believe science has identified many, but not all, of the laws of nature. For instance, I am cer-tain that we have only scratched the surface in the area of intra-body communication, chemical messengers, and the like. I be-lieve that science should study the miraculous functions of the body rather than trying to improve upon or replace these func-tions with external substances like drugs. Religion and science aside, emotions, beliefs, and attitudes hold vital answers to health.

# Walking the Spiritual Path

In Chapter 1, I explained two powers within you—the soul and the spirit. Let's continue with a little more information on the soul. The soul is created by your use of your conscious mind. Your conscious mind is very powerful and has direct control over your attitudes and belief patterns, whether negative or positive. We are all subject to the power of our conscious minds. Whether coping with feelings of helplessness, control issues, or our need to please others, we are really just trying to maintain a balance within our lives. Many people struggling with issues like these develop illness or disease. Our ability to identify and recognize our own power can lead us to good health and eliminate the *cause* for the disease.

I believe that disease is a perfect response by the perfect spiritual intelligence. The spiritual, innate intelligence that func-tions within us for survival responds to our imbalances with this disease or that disease. *Disease is simply the display of symp-toms and functions that automatically occur as a result of the choices you have made with your conscious mind.* Disease pro-longs survival for as long as possible; the alternative to disease is death. When the physical body finally cannot handle the disease any longer, you die. But what if you could eliminate the *cause* of the disease?

I'm telling you that you are in charge of the most powerful preventative medicine available. You can understand the innate spiritual energy and connect, or actually re-connect, with it. I want you to understand how love, forgiveness, prayer, and thought can influence your health and to understand your own abilities and limitations. Don't give up, but *give in* to the spiritual power within you. Know that you are capable of becoming harmonious with this power.

## SOUL PRINCIPLE

*Religion is a feeble attempt to share the sense of God.*
—John Denver

Again, it is not of significance here what religion you practice. As Christians, we believe that Jesus showed us how to be saved. He showed us how to live. He taught us to walk in his footsteps, to follow him and his teachings. It is up to us, individually, to follow the path he blazed for us. If you hold other religious beliefs or belong to another religion, you may deem someone else in this regard. My point is, Jesus was an example of living in harmony with the spiritual energy.

In *The Secret Doctrines of Jesus*, by H. Spencer Lewis, Ph.D., it says, "The path which Jesus pointed out was to be followed by each individual in privacy and silence. Salvation, spiritual development, and divine attunement were personal, individual qualities, not collective or group attainments."[11] We must each seek our spiritual consciousness individually. Realize that man created religion; God did not create religion. God just is. Man created religions in an effort to study God, Allah, Buddha, or whatever you may call your higher power.

At one of my recent health retreats a woman related this story to the group: She said that she had a terrible experience at church when she was very young. She was now in her eighties and this event still plagued her. While at church one Sunday, the preacher pointed his finger at her during his sermon and said,

"You are a sinner." He then went on with his sermon, but she could not hear anything else. She was terrified and totally absorbed with this notion. The feeling she experienced that day stayed with her for the remainder of her life. It created a helplessness within her that she could never overcome.

She said she never told anyone about how this event had negatively affected her life. She asked me what she could do to tackle the feeling she still had regarding this encounter—the feeling that God thought she was a sinner. I thought for a moment, then I explained to her that it was not God who pointed his finger at her, proclaiming her to be a sinner. It was a man who did this to her, albeit a man preaching his religion.

The woman then breathed a sigh of relief and stated that she had never seen the event in this light. She knew what I said to be true. Simply thinking of the experience in this new way changed her feelings about it entirely. She said understanding this actually freed her of unwanted emotional baggage that she had been carrying around with her for over seventy years! She chose to overcome the negative feeling from that event and get on with her life in a manner that would take her closer to the spiritual path.

As I stated earlier, I see the spiritual path as one that shoots straight and intense, like a laser. With our conscious minds we can make choices that either keep us on or cause us to deviate from that path. The diagram below depicts the spiritual path and our possible deviation from it.

As you can see, the spiritual path points upward, toward heaven. The solid vertical arrow indicates infinity

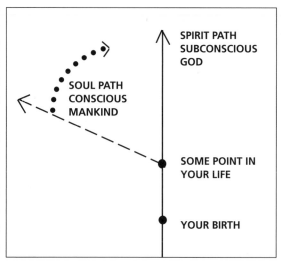

and the true spiritual path. Remember, this path of knowledge and power is unchanging. It never veers, always remaining straight and perfect. We have absolutely no control over this power; we can never affect it. We can dart in and out of the beam or path, but we can never change it.

We are born *on* the path. The dot part way up the spiritual (vertical) arrow indicates an individual person's birth. Once we begin to make conscious choices, we run the risk of leaving the path, because anything other than the perfect innate intelligence (which *is* the path) is contrary to the path.

## SOUL PRINCIPLE

*Straight is the gate, and narrow is the road, that leads to life.*

—Matthew 7:14

The hyphenated arrow depicts the path we, as humans, can create. This path deviates from the true, perfect, innate, spiritual path. The degree of variance is different for each of us. We have the ability to develop a path that leads farther and farther away from the true spirit path with every "wrong" choice we make. Even when we think we are making good conscious choices, we may be interfering with our communication with the spiritual path.

I have been asked many times to write a book to help people with daily living. This book is intended to do just that. By reading this book you have taken a visit to the "thought doctor." And I have a prescription for you. My prescription is a daily Booster Thought. That's right, give yourself one booster thought per day and see if you can turn your power on. See if you can relate to these booster thoughts and apply the lessons they teach to your own life. You can identify just how far from the spiritual path you have roamed and begin to turn your path back toward the spiritual one. Maybe you are quite close, quite happy, and quite healthy. Maybe you are not so close, not so happy, and not so healthy. Whichever is the case, the choices you make are yours, and yours alone. Understand the likelihood that you can communicate with, resonate with, or interfere with this spiritual power.

# PART II

# The Path of Knowledge

## Booster Thoughts, Daily Lessons for Living

The end of learning is to know God, and out of that knowledge to love him, and to imitate him, as we may the nearest, by possessing our souls of true virtue.

—John Milton

# An Introduction to Booster Thoughts

First, I want you to become *aware* of the special power within you. Second, I want you to *believe* you have this power. Third, I want you to *know* you have this power and know how to use it. Finally, I want you to know that *you* are in charge of your health.

As the "thought doctor," I have decided to provide you with some mental prescriptions. Like your regular medical doctor prescribed the better known booster shots, I am now prescribing what I call Booster Thoughts. If I were writing a prescription for their usage it would read something like this: "To be taken mentally once per day." It is my intention that you fully absorb each thought and use each lesson to your advantage. See if you can put yourself in each situation or relate your own experience to the one offered. Some booster thoughts ask you to perform a task while others simply relay a story for you to digest. Some give practical advice. Some may make you laugh; others may make you cry. The object is to get you to realize that you have special powers within you and that you, and only you, can turn those powers on to lead yourself to improved health, vitality, happiness, and success. I want to enlighten you, show you a way, and allow you to fulfill your life as only you can do.

There is a universal consciousness, an abundance of universal energy. Man's soul energy combines with the supreme spirit energy to create a universal pool of power, knowledge, and consciousness. Every living organism contributes to and takes from this pool. As we learn, create, and grow we add new knowledge to the universal pool. Our ability to take from that pool is what enables us to learn, create, and grow. It is a constant give and take of knowledge and energy. Part III will cover this information in greater detail. The point I want to make here is that you may take the information from these Booster Thoughts and use it to learn and grow as an individual, to get closer to the spiritual energy that is within you, the energy that created you and that runs your body at a subconscious level. Tap into your energy to improve your life and your health.

Note that the Booster Thoughts are divided into the three sections—physical, mental, and spiritual. Within each of the sections you will find further divisions according to specific topics. You may want to choose a Booster Thought from the physical plane one day and follow it by one from the mental or spiritual plane the next day. The Booster Thoughts are not given in a prescribed order. It is okay to take them in any order you deem right for you. After all this is over-the-counter medication, or rather, over-the-counter meditation. Keep in mind that even when you think you are all alone facing the stresses of the day, you really are not alone, as you still have the power that made you within you. The Booster Thoughts will enable you to identify with this feeling of power.

CHAPTER 3

# THE PHYSICAL PLANE

> Our body is a machine for living. It is organized
> for that, it is its nature. Let life go on in it
> unhindered and let it defend itself, it will do
> more than if you paralyse it by encumbering it
> with remedies.
>                           —Leo Tolstoy, War and Peace

We live in the physical plane. Bodies, homes, cars, plants, trees, and animals are all physical entities. We can touch, taste, feel, hear, and smell things in this plane. In other words, we can use one or more of our five senses to identify objects in the physical plane. Can you see it? It's physical. Can you touch it? It's physical. You get the picture. Concrete objects, like our bodies, make up the physical plane. In this portion of Booster Thoughts we will address your health on the physical level.

Your current physical condition is a result of the choices you have made in the past. You may have fibromyalgia, ulcers, pain, a cold, or some other disease. Whatever your condition, your physical state today is simply a display of choices you made in the past. Bad choices result in ill health. On the other hand, proper choices result in a healthy physical condition. Eat right, exercise, don't smoke, get plenty of rest, drink pure water, and think happy thoughts to create a healthy physical body. Sounds simple! Well, it really is.

The beautiful part about it is that *you* can change your current physical condition. If you don't like your physical health or body today, you can take charge and change it. Making changes in the choices you make in the Six Essentials for Life (those choices that led you to your current state of health) will literally change your physical condition—for better or for worse. When I state that your past choices have led to your current condition, I am not placing blame or guilt. Nor am I expecting you to blame yourself or feel guilty. I am merely stating the facts as I see them. The key here is to understand, accept, and move on.

If you don't like your current physical condition, set out on a course to change it, by making different choices. If you are currently in ill health, making healthier choices in the Six Essentials for Life will *improve* your physical health. If you eat a steady barrage of junk food, smoke a pack of cigarettes per day, and live in a state of worry about your bills, then chances are your health suffers in some way. Choosing to eliminate or change any or all of these choices will result in improved health. You will physically note a change in your health. On the other hand, if you are currently in good physical condition, but begin to make poor food choices, start smoking, stop exercising, or develop a real hate for your boss, you will negatively impact your physical health.

There is a lot of talk about body/mind/spirit concepts—in that order. However, I see the order differently. I believe the appropriate order to be: *spirit/memory/mind/body*. Your body is the end result of spiritual intelligence, memory, and your soul energy (mind). Your body is literally created by spirit, memory, and mind.

This section is devoted to the physical plane—the physical body that you've always attempted to heal or maintain. In this section, you will find out how others have created disease or health; learn how you can change your life by changing your choices; discover a recipe for physical well-being; and determine that your health is up to you.

# Thoughts on what you eat and drink

### BOOSTER THOUGHT #1
### Are you eating away at your health?

The human body is by far the most sophisticated piece of machinery ever devised. Compared to the body, even the most advanced computers are Tinker Toys. Our bodies' survival mechanisms are designed and constructed in such a way that they can overcome just about anything we do to them—at least for a while. One of the most harmful things we do to our bodies, in my opinion, is to eat too much of the food that keeps our survival systems going full tilt constantly—high protein meat, poultry, fish, grain, and stimulating soft drinks.

The amount of daily recommended protein has changed over the years. Around the end of the nineteenth century, the recommendation was 118 grams of protein a day. By 1965, either our needs or our knowledge had changed. The recommended amount dropped from 118 grams to 70 grams for men and 58 grams for women in the 35- to 75-year-old age group. But it didn't stop there. In the 1970s and 1980s, not only the amount recommended by the U.S. government changed, but the age groupings also changed. The recommendation for men 15 to 51 years old was 56 grams; for 19 to 51 year-old women it was 44 grams. As you can see, the recommended amount keeps dropping. Today, some authorities suggest that our daily protein intake should be limited to 20 grams. This is probably close to ideal. However, as a practical matter, I believe you can get by with up to 40 grams a day as long as all of these protein grams move hand-in-hand through your digestive system with neutralizing fruits and vegetables.

Too much protein and not enough fruits and vegetables will eventually have a debilitating effect on your body or bodily functions. The specific effect will vary from person to person. It may be a stiff neck or upset stomach for you. It may be cancer or the flu for someone else. Here's a little story to illustrate my point.

When I first moved back to the area where I now live, I ran into an old friend who had been a patient of mine years before. I hadn't seen Martha in quite some time. I asked her how she was doing and I got this reply: "Not so good, Dr. Morter. You see, my grandson, Joey, is very ill." Her concern was written in pain across her face.

I said, "Well, tell me about it, Martha." She went on to say that it all began when Joey slid into first base during a baseball game. He hurt his ankle, so they took him to the doctor. They were told it seemed to be a minor sprain, to put ice on it, and to bring him back in a week if it didn't get any better. The ankle just wouldn't seem to heal, so they took him back to see the doctor. After asking lots of questions and performing a routine examination, the doctor asked if he could x-ray Joey's ankle. Joey's dad readily agreed, hoping to find some answers.

And answers they got, as the X-ray revealed that Joey had bone cancer. In fact, his bones were riddled with cancer to the point that the doctor couldn't believe that he could even walk. Furthermore, the doctor recommended that they amputate Joey's leg to increase the chance of getting rid of the cancer, which they did. At this point in the story I said, "Martha, wait right there. Let me guess what Joey eats. I bet he eats nothing but hamburgers and drinks nothing but colas." Then Martha began to cry.

She said, "Dr. Morter, you are so close. He eats hot dogs and drinks diet colas."

I asked her if the doctor had addressed his nutrition at all. She said that he had not. In fact, she had even asked him if Joey's diet was related to his cancer. The doctor told them there was no relation whatsoever between what Joey ate and his cancer.

I said, "Well, I believe that there is. And if his diet is not changed, then he is not ever going to get well. So love him a lot—while you can." After a hug and a thank you, Martha went on her way.

A few months later, I ran into Martha again. One look at her told me that things were still not good. She said that Joey was in the hospital again, that he was really sick and spitting up blood. She explained to me that, as a grandmother, it was very difficult for her to watch her little grandson deteriorate right in front of her eyes. I then told Martha to love little Joey every day, because he was probably not going to be around much longer. I didn't believe he would leave the hospital this time. I suggested she say and do the things with him that she felt good about, because I didn't want her to have any regrets after he was gone. And, sure enough, a couple of weeks later Joey died.

I tell this story, not to make you sad, but because it is so indicative of the problems that can be created by too much acidity in the body. Too much animal protein and too many man-made stimulants that leave the body too far on the acid side of the pH scale can lead to diseases and situations like Joey's. Wouldn't it have been great if Joey's urine and saliva had been tested before the cancer ever developed? If Joey's parents could have known that his diet was making him so acidic that he would eventually develop cancer, don't you think they would have done everything in their power to change his diet? I certainly believe that they would have. How about you, are you eating away at *your* health?

## SOUL PRINCIPLE

*Too much animal protein and too many man-made stimulants that leave the body too far on the acid side of the pH scale, can lead to diseases and/or ill health.*
—Dr. M. T. Morter, Jr.

**BOOSTER THOUGHT #2**
**Take these steps to healthy eating.**
In this day and age it's as easy to be healthy as it is to be sick. Begin on the road to health by giving your body a chance. Give it the best kinds of foods to work with on a regular basis. Here are my recommendations for doing that.

### FOUR STEPS TO HEALTHY EATING

**STEP ONE** to better health is to eat more cooked vegetables every day. For you, one serving a day may be an increase.

**STEP TWO** is to eat fewer high protein foods each day. Eat smaller portions of beef, pork, poultry, and fish, while continuing to add more cooked vegetables to your meals.

**STEP THREE** is not to cook the vegetables quite so much, leave them a bit crunchy (al denté) and add one serving of raw fruit or veggies each day.

**STEP FOUR** is to begin to lessen the amount of sugar, salt, coffee, tea, cola drinks, and processed (man-made) snack foods.

Now, just how quickly should you make these changes? In order to answer that question, you should understand a bit more about the ideal diet. Under ideal conditions, your daily diet (excluding Thanksgiving, Christmas, your birthday, and an assortment of other special days) should consist of a combination of:

45% cooked vegetables and fruits
30% raw fruits and vegetables
25% nuts, grains, seeds, beef, fish, poultry, pork, or
    whatever else

We each follow our own individual eating pattern, so guidelines are general. The following timetable for a transitional diet is suggested for those who have been eating a diet which mainly consists of meats, "fast foods," refined carbohydrates, processed or prepared ready-made foods, and stimulants such as tea, cola, coffee, salt, or alcoholic beverages. Your diet may actually be more healthy than that and may already include lots of fresh, whole foods such as vegetables and fruits. If you know your diet is already somewhat healthy, you may be able to telescope the time periods recommended to better suit your own health needs. However, if you have been putting your body through food abuse for many years, you may need to extend each period a bit longer. How your body responds to each phase in the transitional diet will let you know how fast you can improve your diet or if you need to slow the process. If unpleasant symptoms appear, back off. Go back to eating some of the foods your body is accustomed to, then, once again, slowly eliminate them from your diet.

| TIMETABLE FOR THE TRANSITIONAL DIET | |
|---|---|
| *Phase One:* | Increase the amount of whole foods and cooked vegetables you consume each day. |
| *Phase Two:* <br> *After 3–4 Days* | Add one serving of fruit each day. |
| *Phase Three:* <br><br> *After 2 Weeks* | Make one meal each day fruit and cooked vegetables *only.* <br> Start to cut back on the amount of health inhibitors you regularly consume (for example; coffee, tea, cola drinks). |
| *Phase Four:* <br> *After 3 Weeks* | Start to reduce salt. <br> Add more cooked vegetables and raw fruits. |
| *Phase Five:* <br><br> *After 1 Month* | Start to reduce the amount of high protein foods you eat daily. <br> Decrease your diet by one health inhibitor per week (for example: alcohol, chocolate, cigarettes, fast foods). <br> Start to add raw or lightly cooked vegetables. |
| *Phase Six:* <br><br> *Thereafter* | Continue to decrease the amount of acid-producing foods while increasing the amount of alkaline-producing foods that you consume on a daily basis. (The list of acid-producing and alkaline-producing foods is provided in Lesson 3.) |

Begin today to change your diet by applying the Four Steps to Healthy Eating according to the timetable above. This timetable for a transitional diet is designed to aid you in a gradual change in your diet; each phase in the transitional diet leads to the next one. Changing your diet to a more healthful balance between acid and alkaline producing foods should be done *slowly*.

Even *you* are not an exception to this rule. Quick, radical changes may lead to long-term health, but short-term misery.

# SOUL PRINCIPLE

*Improve your diet by making the changes outlined in the "Timetable for the Transitional Diet."*

—Dr. M. T. Morter, Jr.

**BOOSTER THOUGHT #3**
**Alkaline and Acid Foods: Know the Difference**

---

## ALKALINE PRODUCING FOODS

---

| | | |
|---|---|---|
| Almonds | Dates, dried | Parsnips |
| Apples | Figs, dried | Peaches |
| Apricots | Grapefruit | Pears |
| Avocados | Grapes | Pineapple |
| Bananas | Green beans | Potatoes, sweet |
| Beans, dried | Green peas | Potatoes, white |
| Beet greens | Lemons | Radishes |
| Beets | Lettuce | Raisins |
| Blackberries | Lima beans, dried | Raspberries |
| Broccoli | Lima beans, green | Rutabagas |
| Brussels sprouts | Limes | Sauerkraut |
| Cabbage | Milk, goat's* | Soy beans, green |
| Carrots | Millet | Spinach, raw |
| Cauliflower | Molasses | Strawberries |
| Celery | Mushrooms | Tangerines |
| Chard leaves | Muskmelon | Tomatoes |
| Cherries, sour | Onions | Watercress |
| Cucumbers | Oranges | Watermelon |

---

*Recommended only for infants for whom mother's milk is not available

## NEUTRAL FOODS THAT HAVE AN ACIDIFYING EFFECT

| | | |
|---|---|---|
| Corn oil | Refined sugar | Olive oil |
| Corn syrup | | |

## ACID PRODUCING FOODS

| | | |
|---|---|---|
| Bacon | Currants | Pork |
| Barley | Eggs | Prunes* |
| Beef | Flour, white | Rice, brown |
| Blueberries | Flour, whole wheat | Rice, white |
| Bran, wheat | Haddock | Salmon |
| Bran, oat | Honey | Sardines |
| Bread, white | Lamb | Sausage |
| Bread, whole wheat | Lentils, dried | Scallops |
| Butter | Lobster | Shrimp |
| Carob | Milk, cow's* | Spaghetti |
| Cheese | Macaroni | Squash, winter |
| Chicken | Oatmeal | Sunflower seeds |
| Codfish | Oysters | Turkey |
| Corn | Peanut butter | Veal |
| Corned beef | Peanuts | Walnuts |
| Crackers, soda | Peas, dried | Wheat germ |
| Cranberries | Pike | Yogurt |
| | Plums* | |

*These foods are alkaline-producing but have an acidifying effect on the body.

The concept that foods have acid-producing and alkaline-producing qualities is not brand new. In 1920 Ragnar Berg, a Swedish chemist, published a food list that consisted of all major foods, their calories, protein, fat, carbohydrate, alkaline and acid contents. Dr. R.A. Richardson listed foods by these categories in 1925.[12] So study in this area has been going on for quite some time. I am not the first, nor will I be the last, to research the acid and alkaline properties of foods.

You probably noticed that the alkaline-producing foods are essentially fruits and vegetables and that acid-producing foods are generally meats (poultry, beef, fish), dairy products, and grains. Our bodies are approximately three-fourths alkaline, therefore we need to replenish and refuel them with three-fourths alkaline-producing foods.

## SOUL PRINCIPLE

*Knowing the difference between acid and alkaline foods should play a key role in what you eat.*
—Dr. M. T. Morter, Jr.

### BOOSTER THOUGHT #4
### So, what should I eat?

Learning to eat right may be difficult at first. Following the simple guidelines in Booster Thought #2 should help, but it's really just a matter of choice. You must *choose* to eat right. It's as simple as that, but no one can do it for you. I suggest that you strictly follow the guidelines for the first month or so, then be creative. I am not so rigid that I believe you can never have a piece of chocolate cake or a slice or two of pizza. In fact, I believe that you might want and need to indulge in these simple pleasures periodically, and, if and when you do, enjoy them and be happy for the indulgence. Don't be guilty and woeful for it. (I say this because I know the devastating effects of negative thinking.)

I have seen many vegetarians who actually made themselves ill worrying about their diets or the diets of others. You should not beat yourself up over a trace of animal protein that might be in a particular sauce at a restaurant because this is supposed to be your meal with no protein for the day. Relax, be sensible, and enjoy your meals. As I said before, I believe what you eat five days a week, on the average, determines your level of health. So it's okay to indulge yourself every now and then. Just keep in mind that it's the steady barrage of colas, beer, hamburgers, chocolate, or chips that is detrimental to your health. If you eat plenty of fruits and vegetables, drink pure water, and indulge in your favorite treats only now and then, you will reap the benefits of better health.

# SOUL PRINCIPLE

*The 75%-fruits-and-veggies-and-25%-everything-else rule*
*is the best method for maintaining health and ideal body*
*weight.*

—Dr. M. T. Morter, Jr.

**BOOSTER THOUGHT #5**
**Beware of going on a "fast" or out for "fast food."**
The rigors of diet extremes can be very harmful to your health. Eating a steady stream of junk food can be damaging, but so can the opposite extreme—fasting. I do not recommend fasts, unless monitored closely by a healthcare professional. While there are many benefits that result from fasts, the side effects, unmonitored, can be devastating. Among the side effects you would expect to encounter are severe headaches, nausea, and dizziness. Over the years I have had experience with a variety of fasts, from water fasts to juice fasts. Those on a water fast eat no foods and drink only water. People on a juice fast consume only juice, which is typically pure fruit or vegetable juice.

The goal of most fasts is to cleanse the body, especially the colon. However, this can also be accomplished without fasting. There are some very good colon cleansing products on the market today. When looking for such a product, be sure it is an all-natural product that has not been heat treated.

Another diet extreme that can be damaging to your body is "yo-yo dieting." You probably know what I mean by this. Many people go on a strict diet, reduce calories to a bare minimum, and lose weight quickly. Then, upon reaching the desired goal, they go right back to their old diet, whatever it was, and put all the weight back on (and maybe even add a pound or two). When the "fat" weight is reached again, they go back on the next fad diet to take off those unwanted pounds quickly. And the cycle continues. This up and down, roller-coaster diet scheme can be damaging to your health. Your body was not designed to deal with such dietary stress. While keeping your weight under control is a worthy goal, a series of fad diets is not the preferred method to reach or maintain that goal. A steady, consistent intake of good food will help you to maintain the necessary alkaline reserve, while giving you the energy and vitality you need. In general, alkaline producing foods are low in fat and simple carbohydrates which allow the body to attain its normal weight.

## SOUL PRINCIPLE

*Up and down, roller coaster diet schemes can be damaging to your health.*

—Dr. M. T. Morter, Jr.

# Thoughts on What You Breathe

**BOOSTER THOUGHT #1**
**The importance of the air that you breathe**
We've all heard the expression, "The best things in life are free." Well, nothing is freer than air. However, the quality of air that you breathe is no light matter and needs some careful consideration. You do have a choice in the environmental air that you breathe; you choose where you live and where you work. While it may not be easy to change either of these, moving to a different location or changing jobs may be necessary. Personal circumstances are usually the deciding factor in both of these situations. Picking up your family and possessions and traipsing off to another part of the state or country, or finding a new job, are major steps in anyone's life. However, if you live or work in surroundings that are heavily polluted by industrial or agricultural activity, your body and the bodies of your family members could suffer needlessly.

Recent studies on industrial pollution showed a definite increase in health problems for workers in the dry cleaning business, for example. Studies from Great Britain, Sweden, and the United States reported the rate of miscarriages in women who work in dry cleaning establishments where they are routinely exposed to dry cleaning chemicals is over two times greater than that in pregnant mothers without this exposure. Your decisions about where you live and work *are* a matter of priorities.

You may have more options in your choice of where and how you live and work than you realize. The decision to accept a job in a chemically-laden environment, such as a printing company or the spray painting department of an auto body shop, is a conscious choice; the decision to live in an area of heavy air pollution is also a conscious choice.

Respiratory toxicity from environmental pollution imposes severe stress on the body. That stress can exhaust vulnerable organs and systems of your body, leading to ill health and disease. Evaluate the air you breathe on a regular basis. As a general rule, if you can smell the air and it's a man-made smell, then it is a potential problem. For instance, in your workplace, do you smell chemicals like cleansers or paint? In your home, do you smell cigar or cigarette smoke? If so, then you may want to consider addressing the issue. Breathing in toxic air on a consistent basis will have some effect on you. Your body must deal with this toxic air and it will stress and exhaust you in some manner.

So you need to make the conscious choice to evaluate the air you breathe at home and at work. If at all possible, take the necessary actions to clean up the air that you breathe. If you are unable to change jobs or move away from the environmental air stresses you are under, you may want to consider an air purifier. There are some very good ones available and they come in a variety of sizes and a range of prices. A little research in this area may allow you to breathe a little easier.

## SOUL PRINCIPLE

*The quality of the air you breathe needs careful consideration.*

—Dr. M. T. Morter, Jr.

**BOOSTER THOUGHT #2**
**An exercise in breathing**

Air is one of the most important elements in your life. You can live without food for weeks, without water for days, but you can only live a matter of moments without air. Air contains the fuel we use every second of our lives for releasing energy to our trillions of cells. How well our cells are energized depends, in some part, on how well we breathe. Breathing is one of the most important functions of our bodies. Breathing is under the control of the autonomic system; in other words, it is involuntary. You just do it. It is one of the functions of your subconscious mind, part of the master program. However, you can control your breathing consciously. You can pant, hold your breath, or hyperventilate if you want. You can also take slow, deep, invigorating, revitalizing breaths.

Ancient societies have been said to believe that breath was their instant contact with their gods. The Hindus, perhaps more than any other people, take breathing seriously and have developed it into a vital science. They believe that the good things in life—peace, poise, and longevity—depend upon right breathing. They speak of the air as being, or containing, *prana*, which is the container of "vital spirit." Whether this is so or not, we are hardly in a position to judge. I do believe that deep rhythmic breathing is one of the quickest ways to energize tired bodies.

For centuries, societies have studied breathing. In England, Austria, France, and Germany during the early part of the twentieth century, there were schools, sanitariums, and doctors teaching diaphragmatic breathing, as a part of their regular treatments. This deep-belly breathing has been found to energize and oxygenize the body in a more complete way. Try this little exercise in deep breathing that I found in *Be Happier, Be Healthier* by Gayelord Hauser.[13]

Wear something that fits loosely around the neck and waist or something elasticized. Lie down and relax. Now, breathe in slowly and gently through your nose and don't force yourself. Then, exhale through your mouth. As you exhale, hum the letter U. Exhale for as long as possible, without forcing. Now take a watch and time your inhalation and your exhalation.

A study done by Dr. Tirala of Vienna in the 1940s revealed that the average person could only inhale for ten or fifteen seconds and could exhale for even less.[14] If you found that you fit into this category, you might like to try to increase the length of time you inhale and exhale as you perform this little exercise. Learn to do some deep-belly breathing. Lie down and take a deep breath, concentrating on filling your belly (which is actually open-ing your diaphragm). You should feel your abdomen round out and your chest expand. Do this consciously as many times as it takes to get the full feel of this nostril-to-belly inhalation.

Of course, the flip side of inhalation is exhalation. You can't have one without the other. Exhalations are very important, too. The deeper and longer you exhale, the more impurities you re-move from your lungs and the more relaxed your whole body becomes. Think of your exhaling breaths as house-cleaning breaths. For the purpose of our deep-belly breathing exercise, we are going to follow Mr. Hauser's suggestion of exhaling through the mouth while humming the letter U.

So, it goes like this: take a deep-belly breath in through the nose for as along as possible. Then exhale out through the mouth while humming the letter U for as long as possible. Now add one more thing to this exercise—a positive affirmation. Think some-thing positive while you practice your deep breathing.

Dr. Tirala suggested practicing deep breathing once a day for ten or fifteen minutes. Others have suggested similar prac-tices. I think that five minutes per day of practiced, deep-belly breathing will help you physically, as well as mentally, if you think positive affirmations while practicing your breathing. A good time to do this exercise might be in the evening, just before going to sleep. In addition, when you get especially stressed or tense dur-ing the day, take a few deep-belly breaths to pump some extra oxygen throughout your body. Take notice of how you are breath-ing right now. You may find that just by reading about breathing, you are breathing more deeply.

## SOUL PRINCIPLE

*Practice deep breathing while thinking positive affirmations.*
—Dr. M. T. Morter, Jr.

# Thoughts on How You Exercise

**BOOSTER THOUGHT #1**
**Exercise is not selfish**

Lack of exercise seems to be part of a national, if not universal, social change. Most people these days simply do not get enough exercise. Most of us perform jobs that aren't physical enough to count as exercise, which is why most Americans are not in very good physical shape. Sure, there's an exercise and fitness craze running rampant across the nation, but let's face it, the majority of America is not into it.

According to government surveys, less than twenty-five percent of us are as active as we should be. More than half of us are almost "completely sedentary." And this is at our own admission! A sedentary lifestyle has been linked to as many as 250,000 deaths per year, or about twelve percent of all deaths. The Centers for Disease Control and Prevention has declared an "epidemic of physical inactivity," which is just as detrimental to health as smoking and high cholesterol levels. Over fifty percent of Americans are overweight, which is twice as many as in the 1970s.[15] Now that's scary!

One survey revealed that seventy-three percent of women don't exercise enough, and older women (over 65) were the most likely to fit into this category. When asked to list the benefits of exercise, those who answered one survey cited the following benefits: improved overall health, better chance for success at maintaining ideal weight, improved cardiovascular function, better mental outlook, more energy, and better chance for losing weight.[16] The link between most of these benefits and exercise has been proven over and over again. We know these to be the benefits, yet we still choose to be couch potatoes.

The challenge here, for all Americans, is to become more active. Our lives are all very busy. We have to commute to work, cook dinner, car-pool kids here and there, attend to family matters, and the list goes on. However, we all seem to find time to do the things we think are most important. If the President of the United States can find the time to jog three or four times a week, then surely anyone can find time for some increased physical activity.

For most people it's simply a matter of making choices and changes, and determining priorities that place your health first. This does not constitute being selfish, but being healthy. Think about it like this: being and staying healthy is actually in the best interests of those you love. If you do not maintain your health, you may not be around much longer. Taking an interest in your health, including a little exercise, is something you can do for yourself and your loved ones.

I am reminded here of a time when I talked with an over-weight patient, Sam, about including an exercise program in his life. He said he just didn't have time to exercise. He was a busy, forty-year-old corporate executive who got to the office at 7:30 in the morning, six days a week. He worked all day long, often eating lunch out of the vending machines at the office, and didn't arrive home until about 7:00 each evening.

This father had a sixteen-year-old son who was having trouble in algebra and he explained that he needed the time in the evening to help his son with his school work. To Sam, his son's grades were directly linked to his son's future success. In addition, he felt that spending quality time with his teenage son was very important. As you can guess, he strongly resisted my suggestion that he use some time in the evening to exercise.

To get my point across, we did a quick review of Sam's health records. It became glaringly obvious to Sam that if he didn't change something in his life, he wasn't going to have much of a life left. He realized that if he didn't act a bit "selfishly" by taking the time to exercise that he would not be around much longer to be a father to his son. At least not the type of father he wanted to be.

When Sam realized that he had to make some changes, he began to outline some alternatives to his regular schedule. Where could he find some time in his day? He could get up at 5:00 in the morning, when it was still dark outside; go to the gym instead of eating any lunch; work out after helping his son with algebra; skip dinner; or hire a tutor for his son after school and ask his son to work out with him in the evenings.

Sam chose the latter alternative. This ensured his son's academic success, while allowing him to spend the quality time with his son that he desired. My point is that you have to make a conscious decision to block out time to take care of your health, including time to exercise. We each have our own special circumstances, but when you really want to, you can find a way to do the things you think are important. Make the same commitment to exercise that you do to eating. Just do it.

## SOUL PRINCIPLE

*Take time to take care of your health, including time to exercise.*

—Dr. M. T. Morter, Jr.

**BOOSTER THOUGHT #2**
**Take a walk in the park**

Taking a stroll in the park, through the woods, or across the meadow has many natural benefits. If done at a brisk pace, you get a little needed exercise. When done in the name of peace-of-mind you get some mental therapy. If the air is clean and pure, you oxygenate your lungs and body. I highly recommend walking in the great outdoors, enjoying nature's bounty. I'm talking about a walk in a place where the air is clean and pure, not down a city street filled with bumper-to-bumper cars emitting noxious fumes.

If you live in the city, you may have a park that you can walk in or you may have to drive out of town. The benefits are worth it and I suggest that you do this on a regular basis. If you live in the suburbs or a smaller town, then your very own neighborhood may serve the purpose. However or wherever you decide to take your stroll, relax and enjoy it.

You should walk in a manner that adds to your bodily balance. In other words, when your right foot is forward, your left arm should be forward; when your left foot is forward, your right arm should be forward. This contralateral movement coordinates and balances your body while you walk.

In addition, don't wear a headset to pipe in rock and roll, rap, the weather report, or your favorite morning talk show host.

Instead, play your thoughts and listen carefully to them. Yes, think. This is a great time to get in touch with your soul. You can use this time to give thanks and show your gratitude to the almighty creator, to make plans for reaching your next goal, or for some other positive mental activity. *Positive* is the operative word here. If you can't come up with something positive to think about, then just walk along thinking this, "Thank you for my perfect health. Thank you for my perfect happiness. Thank you for my perfect success." Just think this over and over. You will begin to feel good. As you walk and think positive thoughts you strengthen your mind and body and the relationship between them. Walk on.

## SOUL PRINCIPLE

*Taking a leisurely walk through your neighborhood or park, while thinking positive, uplifting thoughts is an excellent way to stay connected and balanced in soul and spirit.*

—Dr. M. T. Morter, Jr.

### BOOSTER THOUGHT #3
### The weekend warrior

You have probably heard the term "weekend warrior"—the warrior who only performs at "special battles." The scenario goes something like this. Lie around all week long, watching TV while eating a whole bag of chips each evening. Then, come the weekend, hop out there to shovel the new three-foot-high snow from your 100-foot-long driveway. Or say "Yes!" to the guys who want to play a game of full-tackle football at the park. Or arrive at the company picnic to find that you have been named activity chairman for the girls, and the guy you're in competition with for a promotion has been named activity chairman for the boys. The first activity is a softball game. Feeling the need to show some company spirit, you, of course, play the whole game, followed by a game of volleyball, badminton, and croquet. To top it off, you compete in the tug-of-war, sack hop, and wheelbarrow race.

Does this sound familiar to you? Have you ever done anything like this? Most of us have. Your body seems to rise to the occasion while you are performing your seemingly simple feats, but it always lets you know within a day or two that you have overdone it. You get so stiff and sore that you can hardly move. So stiff, in fact, that you decide not to do such a foolish thing ever again—a decision that only lasts until you get challenged to participate in a walk-a-thon to raise money for the local orphanage or to take a bike ride on the new trail out by the lake, when, of course, you hop to it and do it again. The point is, if you were in good physical shape, then performing these somewhat minor bouts of activity would not pose a problem for you. You wouldn't wake in the morning so sore that you couldn't get out of bed or bend over to tie your shoes. You would be able to play a game of sports or ride the bike trail and go right on with your life as if you had merely walked to the back yard to pick some flowers.

Does that sound better to you? If so, including a regular exercise program in your life may help you to accomplish that goal. It might help you perform these innocuous tasks without the full-scale soreness and pains associated with the common "weekend warrior" routine. Even a bit of exercise, on a regular basis, will get you to a higher level of fitness and better health.

### SOUL PRINCIPLE

*I will exercise regularly.*

—Dr. M. T. Morter, Jr.

# Thoughts on How You Rest

**BOOSTER THOUGHT #1**
**A matter of emotion**

When it comes to rest and sleep, a more thorough explanation is given in Chapter 1, "The Powers Within You." At this time I'd like to address a specific sleep-related issue that plagues many today—insomnia. This condition is quite prevalent in our society. It is my belief that neither a sleeping pill nor a wake-up pill is necessary. In a normal healthy condition, no one should have to resort to this measure in order to get adequate sleep or to wake from a restful period of sleep. If you are in a constant state of agitation that does not allow you to sleep, then you must address what is causing you to be this way.

Remember the example of the bear in the cave and how it relates to emotional memory override? As a reminder, when your ancestor approached his cave to find that it was occupied by a bear, he had two physical choices—fight or run. The fight or flight reflex is brought on by an acute, or sudden, happening. (He walked into the cave, saw the bear, experienced fear, and either fought or ran.) He didn't question; he didn't think. There was just instantaneous reaction on the subconscious level. In this instance, the causative factor was a physical one—an actual bear. In addition, the whole experience, from sighting the bear to producing adrenaline internally for either fighting or running, was over in a matter of seconds. This example depicts the way the human body was designed to function. We are programmed to respond to threats on the physical level in order to survive.

The problem enters when we produce threats to our safety on a mental level. In other words, we live in a state of fear, stress, hate, jealousy, regret, anger, or any other such negative emotion. These negative emotions produce chemicals to which the body must respond. Living under a cloud of any of these negative emotions, or any combination of them, on a daily basis results in exhaustion. The target of this exhaustion varies from person to person. While one person may experience the exhaustion of a single organ, the next may find that an entire system of the body becomes exhausted. Still others may get colds or the flu frequently. Some may develop allergies, while some show signs of bursitis or arthritis. I believe that we actually *earn* these ailments by our negative emotional thinking.

The point is that negative emotions, produced in the mental plane, stimulate chemical production within the body, to which the body must react in the physical plane. A constant production of internal chemicals and internal reactions leads to the exhaustion of the body or some part, or parts, of the body. This is subconscious emotional memory override and we are all capable of placing ourselves in this state.

How does this relate to rest and sleep? Often, when you are

experiencing subconscious emotional memory override you will be unable to sleep. The constant barrage of negative feelings doesn't allow for a calm state of mind, and thus prohibits you from falling asleep. It seems ironic: while your body is experiencing extreme exhaustion, you can't go to sleep. Instead, those in this mental turmoil tend to lie awake fighting their mental battles until the wee hours of the morning. At that point, they may drift off into a fitful bout of sleep—a sleep plagued by these intense negative feelings. When this happens, the deep-rooted negative emotions are actually locked into the memory and mind. They are super glued to the psyche, causing interference in the smooth flow of energy within the body.

Upon awakening, the body is as tired as it was when it went to bed. So, even if a few hours of sleep were accomplished, no resting took place. The body was not able to rejuvenate or recuperate, which should be the major function during sleep. In order for someone to overcome subconscious emotional override and the resulting sleep deprivation, they must address the cause of their negative emotions. Whether the cause is an experience that occurred twenty-five years ago or something that happened last week, getting to the cause is the answer.

You can take positive mental action steps by identifying the culprit in your specific case. Figure out what event or experience initially caused you to feel the way you do. There might be an experience from your childhood that may have resulted in an emotion that is similar to one you are feeling now. In other words, a current experience may be triggering an underlying strong emotion from your past. Once you can identify the main negative emotion that is running your body, then you can begin to face it head on. Following the steps of the forgiveness formula outlined in Part II, "The Mental Plane," will serve as relief. You may find that, in addition, you need to seek the counsel or guidance of a professional. Turning to a minister or other member of the clergy often helps. You may feel the need to seek the advice of a psychologist or other healthcare provider.

The technique I have developed over the past thirty-five years assists people in addressing the cause of their health challenges. Many people who attend my health retreats realize after they arrive that the true cause of their ailment is emotionally based. We work to physically remove the interference caused by the strong negative emotions that have been stored in subconscious memory. When this is done, miracles happen. Understand that I am not claiming to perform miracles. Far from it. The power of God, the spirit, that resides within each of us is responsible for all miracles. By physically unleashing the flow of this divine energy force within us people are able address the subconscious memory and display their full potential. It is very exciting to see people turn on the powers within themselves. I marvel at the unfolding each and every time and I thank God daily for the opportunity to serve him and my fellow man through these retreats.

## SOUL PRINCIPLE

*Falling to sleep thinking positive thoughts will lead to a
better night's rest.*

—Dr. M. T. Morter, Jr.

**BOOSTER THOUGHT #2**
**A time of restoration**

It is during the hours that we sleep that we are able to reju- venate. This rest period is designed to allow for the body to re- build cells and tissues, restore the chemical and hormonal bal- ance, and otherwise rebuild the organs and systems of the body. It is a restorative state that is necessary for the healthy survival of the whole. Not only is the body able to rejuvenate during this rest period, but also the soul. The hours our body is under the control of the subconscious mind allow for the open communi- cation between our soul and the spirit. This is one more reason for going to sleep in a peaceful, loving state.

When you go to sleep after a meditation session or prayer of thanksgiving, you are actually providing an open channel between your soul and the divine spiritual energy. You are allowing for the free flow of energy within you. Sleep is much like a suspen- sion bridge between the soul and the spirit. It can serve to actu- ally link the two energetic levels. Have you ever been seeking the answer to a challenging question to find that it comes to you in your sleep? Maybe in a dream; maybe in the form of a direct answer to your question. This occurs because you have entered the rest period in a positive, energetic state. You have opened yourself to this harmonic level of awareness, even in your subconscious.

It has been said that all prayers are answered. I believe that many times the answers to our prayers come to us during the period of sleep and rest. The key to hearing the answer lies in preparing yourself for the communication prior to going to sleep and then in knowing what the answer means. Our dreams, which often hold the answers to our prayers, may present these answers in an allegoric manner, in other words, expressing the answers by means of symbolic fictional figures and actions. These dreams may seem confusing or surreal to one who has not reached the higher level of consciousness, but to those who are in harmony on a spiritual level the answers are revealed and quite obvious.

Whether you are seeking answers or knowledge, striving to reach a higher level of consciousness or merely plodding through life in an effort to get by from day to day, sleep and rest are imperative. Your body and soul simply require sleep. While the physical needs and amount of sleep time necessary vary from one person to the next, no one is exempt from the need for a period of restoration and rejuvenation. In Genesis 2:2 it says, "By the seventh day God had finished the work he had been doing; so on the seventh day he rested from all his work. And God blessed the seventh day and made it holy, because on it he rested from all the work of creating that he had done."

## SOUL PRINCIPLE

*Sleep and rest are nature's way of restoring the body and the soul.*

—Dr. M. T. Morter, Jr.

# Thoughts on Disease

### BOOSTER THOUGHT #1
### Is my disease or pain caused by a lack of medication?

Reasoning might cause you to arrive at a "yes" answer to this question. If you think about the fact that your pain goes away when you take pain medication, then logic might dictate that the pain was due to a lack of medication. I mean, your thirst is due to lack of fluids. If you get thirsty and take a drink, the thirst goes away; lack of water was the cause of your thirst. Hunger is a result of lack of food. When you are hungry and you eat, the hunger subsides; lack of food was the cause of your hunger. So, with those principles in place, you might reason that pain is caused by lack of medication, since your pain goes away when you take a pain medication. Right? Wrong. I don't think this reasoning could be farther from the truth.

We need to evaluate the role of medicine in health. Medicine actually addresses the *symptoms* of the disease, but rarely the *cause* of the disease. Pain is not the cause of disease, but medication addresses pain. To truly treat the disease, you must find the cause for the disease, find out why you got the disease in the first place. Why did your pain or disease develop? If you can find the cause, then you can treat the cause and attempt to eliminate the disease altogether.

To further the analogy, we don't develop cancer because of a lack of chemotherapy or surgery and we don't get headaches due to a lack of aspirin. So you need to address what happened within your body to cause your pain or disease. Furthermore, what is on your mind when you have a headache or pain or when you think about your particular disease? How do you *feel* about it? You might feel mad, frustrated, or angry about your specific ailments. I've had patients say their pain really made them mad because they couldn't play golf or swim. I've had patients who felt upset and worried by their aches or diseases. Others have expressed aggravation, frustration, guilt, embarrassment, vulnerability, or fear. The point is that you need to address how you really *feel* about your health challenges.

Whatever you *feel* about the condition is the cause for the condition. Your health is an expression of that suppressed feeling. Anger, guilt, bitterness, infidelity, abandonment, rejection, dread, shame, spitefulness, revenge, pride, ridicule, and a myriad of other feelings that are suppressed within you can actually manifest themselves in disease, pain, or discomfort on the physical level. In fact, I have developed a "Feelings Chart" (see below) that lists both positive and negative feelings that may affect health in an adverse way. Identifying which emotions you feel when you think about your pain or disease will help to pinpoint the *cause* of your condition.

Is this to say that you should never take an aspirin for a headache? No, but keep in mind that you are simply treating the pain of the headache; you are not addressing why you got the headache. Also, be aware of the side effects of the medications you take. I recently had a patient call to say that he had been told by his medical doctor that his liver and kidneys were shot. I asked him what he had done to destroy these organs. He then told me that he had taken thirteen Ibuprofen tablets every day for thirteen years to control the pain that resulted from his fibromyalgia. In my opinion, taking the Ibuprofen for the first week or so, until the cause of the pain had been identified, might have been reasonable. However, taking any pain medication on a regular basis for years is ridiculous to me, simply because I see this as "symptom chasing." No amount of medication will *cure* any disease. Medication may make the symptoms go away, but it won't get to the cause of the condition. Disease is not caused by a lack of medication.

## SOUL PRINCIPLE

*Medication addresses symptoms, not causes; and no pain or disease is caused by lack of medication.*

—Dr. M. T. Morter, Jr.

# NEGATIVE FEELINGS

**1**

**A**
| | |
|---|---|
| 1. LONELINESS | 6. SELFISH |
| 2. EMBARRASSMENT | 7. INDECISIVE |
| 3. DEPRESSION | 8. DOMINATING |
| 4. ANGER | 9. COMPULSIVE |
| 5. ANXIETY | 10. JUDGEMENT |

**B**
| | |
|---|---|
| 1. GUILT | 6. GREEDY |
| 2. REGRET | 7. RUTHLESS |
| 3. INADEQUACY | 8. HATEFUL |
| 4. APATHY | 9. GIVING |
| 5. BOREDOM | 10. CRITICAL |

**C**
| | |
|---|---|
| 1. DESPAIR | 6. REJECTING |
| 2. SELF-PITY | 7. DOUBTFUL |
| 3. GRIEF | 8. DISHONEST |
| 4. REMORSE | 9. IMMORAL |
| 5. REJECTION | 10. CYNICAL |

**D**
| | |
|---|---|
| 1. DREAD | 6. RESIGNED |
| 2. SHAME | 7. SPITEFUL |
| 3. IMPATIENCE | 8. FRUSTRATED |
| 4. PERSECUTED | 9. OBSESSIVE |
| 5. ENVY | 10. WORRIED |

**E**
| | |
|---|---|
| 1. IRRITATION | 6. UPSET |
| 2. JEALOUSY | 7. PRIDE |
| 3. POWERLESSNESS | 8. VULNERABLE |
| 4. RESENTMENT | 9. KILL |
| 5. HURT | 10. DEATH |

**F**
| | |
|---|---|
| 1. FEAR | 6. DESTRUCTIVE |
| 2. UNLOVED | 7. AFFAIR |
| 3. ABANDONED | 8. GRUDGE |
| 4. ABUSED | 9. BITTERNESS |
| 5. SUBMISSIVE | 10. SUSPICION |

**G**
| | |
|---|---|
| 1. INFIDELITY | 6. PARANOIA |
| 2. HUNGER | 7. SEX |
| 3. CONTRADICT | 8. RIDICULE |
| 4. ARGUMENTATIVE | 9. DEMANDING |
| 5. FIGHT | 10. REPULSIVE |

# POSITIVE FEELINGS

**2**

**A**
| | |
|---|---|
| 1. CREATIVE | 6. LOVE |
| 2. SENSITIVE | 7. JOY |
| 3. INSPIRED | 8. PEACE |
| 4. IMAGINATIVE | 9. SERENITY |
| 5. FAITHFUL | 10. COMPASSION |

**B**
| | |
|---|---|
| 1. HOPEFUL | 6. SINCERITY |
| 2. ENTHUSIASTIC | 7. HARMONY |
| 3. CONTENTED | 8. COMPATIBILITY |
| 4. ACCEPTING | 9. CONSISTENCY |
| 5. EXPECTANCY | 10. FAITHFULNESS |

**C**
| | |
|---|---|
| 1. PLEASURABLE | 6. GRACIOUS |
| 2. BLISS | 7. LOYAL |
| 3. ELATION | 8. TRUE |
| 4. ENJOYMENT | 9. DEDICATED |
| 5. FULFILLMENT | 10. STEADFAST |

**D**
| | |
|---|---|
| 1. AGREEABLE | 6. UNWAVERING |
| 2. GLAD | 7. FIRM |
| 3. GRATIFIED | 8. CONSCIENTIOUS |
| 4. SATISFIED | 9. STABLE |
| 5. PLEASED | 10. CAREFUL |

**E**
| | |
|---|---|
| 1. JOVIAL | 6. RELIABLE |
| 2. ADORE | 7. TRUST |
| 3. DEVOTION | 8. GOOD |
| 4. BIRTH | 9. DEPENDABLE |
| 5. WARMTH | 10. HONEST |

**F**
| | |
|---|---|
| 1. CHERISH | 6. TRUTHFUL |
| 2. INTIMACY | 7. MORAL |
| 3. FRIENDSHIP | 8. VIRTUOUS |
| 4. PASSION | 9. ACCURATE |
| 5. BENEVOLENT | 10. EXACT |

**G**
| | |
|---|---|
| 1. TRANQUILITY | 6. DELIGHT |
| 2. QUIETNESS | 7. RIGHT |
| 3. CALM | 8. PERFECTION |
| 4. COMPOSURE | 9. SEX |
| 5. DESIRE | 10. HAPPINESS |

**BOOSTER THOUGHT #2**
**Does my lifestyle affect my health?**

The answer to this question is an unequivocal yes! Every choice you make affects your health. Remember the Six Essentials for Life? They are: what you eat, what you drink, how you exercise, how you rest, what you breathe, and what you think. The combination of your choices in these six areas *are* your lifestyle and the choices you make in these six areas have a direct impact on your health.

As I've said before, and wish to reemphasize, your health today is actually the result of your past conscious choices in the Six Essentials for Life. Your lifestyle directly affects your health and may even interfere with the natural functioning of your body. Poor choices made continually (bad habits) cause your body to respond. Keep in mind this natural, innate response is perfect for your survival. If you smoke three packs of cigarettes a day for twenty years, chances are greater that you will develop health problems. One person might develop lung cancer, while another could develop heart problems. But whether the body develops cancer or heart disease is not the point here. The point is that the body is merely trying to survive. The cancer or heart condition is the result of smoking for a prolonged period of time. The alternative to developing heart disease or cancer is immediate death.

To improve your health, you may need to improve your lifestyle. This could mean breaking some habits, which is not so easy to do. Typically, we enjoy doing the activity involved in our bad habits. So to break a bad habit you must stop doing something that you like to do. Bad habits might involve activities that taste good, smell good, feel good, or generally make one feel better. Breaking these habits may be challenging, but rest assured the benefits will be worth it. When you change your lifestyle, you will change your health. This is true on a negative or a positive level. So, *improve* your lifestyle to *improve* your health. You can do it.

# SOUL PRINCIPLE

*Every choice you make affects your health.*
—Dr. M. T. Morter, Jr.

## BOOSTER THOUGHT #3
### Why do children get cancer?

How can an eight-year-old think badly enough or eat poorly enough to create cancer? How can it be that a ten-year-old can have bone cancer, which might even go away only to come back in the blood or the lungs? How can these precious little beings have made such poor choices in the Six Essentials for Life to have caused them to get cancer?

When we are born we inherit certain characteristics that we call genetics. I have come to realize that genetics are an effect. Energetics are the cause. In other words, the energy that created you is the reason that you are the way you are. Each of us was a spiritual or energy being before we were a physical being. We had information in our field that created our genetics. It is logical that if, before we were a physical one-cell being, the information in our energy/spiritual field contained our IQ information, hair color, eye color, sex, size, and such, then it may also have contained other information. Some of that information may have been negative, which under the proper conditions would manifest in disease. So, we could have inherited all of this information from the universal consciousness. It was the information in our field before our physical birth that may have caused cancer, arthritis, diabetes, and any other physical condition known.

Why don't we all have these diseases? I like to think of the mind as an attractor. If we do have negative feelings, as we have discussed, we will attract negative energy from the field. That may manifest as disease. On the other hand (at the risk of over-simplifying) positive feelings and thoughts help to maintain good health.

As I see it, children get serious diseases for a variety of reasons. First, they may inherit the tendency— not the gene, but the *information*—for the disease or ailment from the energy of their creative field. Second, negative information could have come from the mother's field. When we are born we are an extension of our mother. We have been developed inside of our mother and inside of our mother's field. For example, if a mother does not want to be pregnant, then the feelings toward the developing embryo would certainly not be ideal. This can and has caused serious problems in infants since the beginning of time. I find that many times conditions—not even as serious as cancer, but even something like colic—can be caused by the mother being upset. If an infant is sick, the mother may need to identify what is upsetting her.

The child and mother are tuned in to one another. This is so apparent when the nursing mother gets up and walks into the sleeping baby's room to find her just waking up. They both know it is time for the baby to nurse. This phenomena is quite common among nursing mothers.

Fathers are not off the hook here, though, because often it is the father who upsets the mother. So, we all have responsibility in the health arena. I find in working with sick children that the mother or father will have the same spiritual interference as the child. The whole family sometimes has to address the interference in order for the child to show improvement. The mother and father need to help the child work through illnesses with positive energy until the child is able to create her own positive force.

The third cause for serious health challenges in infants is the result of birth trauma, mainly from the misuse of forceps. While there may be other causes of childhood diseases, these have been obvious in my practice. As parents we become anxious when our children get sick. We are quick to blame germs and get antibiotics in an attempt to solve the problem. In my experience in working with children, the ailment may return when antibiotics are discontinued. All I am suggesting is that while you are addressing the condition, you begin to focus on the cause of the illness.

Even though I tell you that your tendency for disease may have come from the information in the field that created you, you are not responsible for the shortcomings of your ancestors. Christians believe that Jesus told us this and to have faith in him.

As a parent, there are positive mental steps you can take. First, you need to be thankful for the miracle of life. Expectant mothers who are thankful for the pregnancy from the moment they learn of it have a positive influence on the development of the baby.

It's easier to blame genetics than it is to take responsibility for our energetics. As a mother or father, learn to see the good in your perfect infant—even when she is sick. If she has gotten off of the spiritual path for some reason, she may need help energetically, not medically. She may need encouragement, love, and positive thoughts to help get her back on the natural, spiritual path. Now, keep in mind that all the positive encouragement in the world is not enough if you don't remove the interference that caused the problem in the first place. As I've taken this journey through life, I've come to realize that we must pass through three steps in order to do that.

First, we must be in a state of awareness. We must become aware of this perfect spiritual power. Second, we must believe in this power. Third, we must know that the power that created us is the only power that can heal us. It is in this state of 'knowingness' that one has reached the highest level of consciousness. Faith is not thinking that God can solve a problem, but knowing that he will.

Mothers of young children need to be positive and thankful in order to raise the healthiest child possible. Does this mean that every sick child is that way because of the mother? Absolutely not. Remember, energetics also plays a role in each person's health. The energy in your field, which was there before you were one cell old, has a direct affect on your health.

Here's an intense thought. The energy of your great-great-great-grandmother on your mother's side and the energy of your great-great-grandfather on your father's side may come together in the formation of you to create a weakness or tendency for disease if it is not neutralized by the love and positive energy of your current surroundings. Most people don't even know that this phenomenon exists; therefore, they do not realize that they can impact their lives and health by overcoming this tendency for disease with the power of positive feelings and the belief that the power within them can heal them. Not only that, these positive feelings will improve the energy you leave in the universal information, thus affecting future generations of your family. If your body can heal a cut or broken bone, why can't it heal cancer and other diseases? I *know* that it can.

## SOUL PRINCIPLE

*Energetics play a key role in our development and state of health.*

—Dr. M. T. Morter, Jr.

# Dr. Morter's Belief Builders
## PRESCRIPTIONS FOR THE PHYSICAL PLANE

- Every living thing has an energy field.
- Every cell of my body is replaced, some hourly.
- My physical body is an expression of my spiritual field.
- We were all created from the same universal energy source.
- Successful people do consistently what unsuccessful people seldom do.
- Doctors are in charge of my disease; I am in charge of my health.
- My current physical condition is a result of all of the choices I have made in the past.
- What I eat and drink, how I exercise and rest, what I breathe and what I think have direct effects on my physical condition.
- Disease is not caused by lack of medication.
- Every disease is the expression of an unlearned lesson.
- Make choices, make changes, take charge.

# CHAPTER 4

# THE MENTAL PLANE

**I find, by experience, that the mind and the body are more than married, for they are most intimately united; and when the one suffers, the other sympathizes.**
—Philip Dormer, Stanhope, Lord Chesterfield

This portion of Booster Thoughts is devoted to the mental plane—thoughts, thought processes, what and how you think, and how it affects your health. You've probably heard the expression, "What you think about you bring about." Well, I believe this to be true. How about this one? "As a man thinketh in his heart, so is he." Yes, thinking and thoughts have a direct impact on our health.

Do you believe you have control over your thoughts? If so, then you should also know that you have control over your health. You use your mind all day long; you constantly think about something. Even when you sleep, your mind is at work—at a subconscious level. The feelings, emotions, and attitudes that you have created in your mind affect your health. Negative feelings are detrimental to your health, while positive ones are beneficial.

Emotional memory override and subconscious emotional memory override (as explained in Chapter 2) are conditions that you create in your mind. This is a state of being in which emotions that come from memory actually determine your physiology. Constantly living in a state of subconscious emotional memory override is exhausting to your body as well as your mind. Who puts you into subconscious emotional memory override? You do. You do it with your mind. Your emotions, which are thoughts mixed with feelings, create chemicals in your body that force a physiological, systemic, or organic survival response—a defense physiology. This constant state of defense physiology exhausts and weakens you, resulting in ill health or disease.

You can actually hate yourself into poor health. You can worry yourself sick. You can allow jealousy to consume you. Your thoughts can actually eat away at your health. On the other hand, you can lift your spirit and strengthen your soul by thinking positive, loving, forgiving thoughts. Read the following Booster Thoughts, placing yourself in each situation. Follow the lessons on the mental plane to learn how you can treat yourself to better health, partly by believing that you can. To become a thoroughly good person, sound in mind and body, is to strengthen your soul by allowing God's wisdom to penetrate your being. As John Maxwell says, "You are only an attitude away from success." I further believe that you are only an attitude away from good health and happiness.

# Thoughts on Happiness

### BOOSTER THOUGHT #1
### Is someone or something else in charge of my life?

Sometimes we think that is true. However, it is just not so. No one else is in charge of your life. You and only you can make the decisions and choices that affect and guide your life. Often people think that their life and happiness are dependent on their mate. If you love your mate and want to please him or her, it may seem that your mate is in charge. Living your life according to someone else's demands may seem to place them in charge; however, it is your choice to live your life that way. So ultimately, you are still in charge of that decision, thus you are still in charge of your life.

Furthermore, no doctor, minister, priest, rabbi, chiropractor, massage therapist, or nutritionist is in charge of your life. No one but you is in charge of your life. This does not mean that these people do not or cannot *affect* your life. It simply means that they are not in *control* of your life. You may have confidence in them, but you must realize that your life is not directly dependent on them. Seeking counsel from a respected individual is perfectly all right, as long as you know you are the one in control of your own life, health, happiness, and success. If you do not like the direction your life is taking, then you may need to make some changes. It is never too late to change, to redirect your life.

Some people even think that some *thing*, not someone, is in charge of their lives. What is the culprit? Germs. Some people blame germs for their health problems. Tiny, microscopic germs, so small they can't even see them without the aid of a microscope. Those that fear germs believe they are a victim of germs, that germs control their lives. They are afraid to touch door knobs, pay phones, and other public properties. These people hide themselves away, locked in a world of fear, behind a mask for protection. This may seem bazaar or radical to you, but it is very real for those that live this way. I have had patients who came in wearing masks and gloves because they were afraid to breathe the air or touch anything that they hadn't washed themselves. Now you may be thinking, "Well, it sounds like the germs *are* in charge of these people's lives." Actually, these people are still in charge; they are just choosing to give germs power. They are choosing to live their lives in fear.

As you live each minute, each hour, each day be aware that you are choosing your lifestyle, that you are forming your being. You and only you are in charge of your life. You will leave this life just as you came into it—alone. It was a glorious moment when you came into this world. You must lead your life so that it will be just as glorious when you leave by making choices each day that will connect you to the healthy, harmonious, spiritual path. *Know* that you are in charge. A successful life is one lived in such a way that everyone you meet between birth and death is glad they met you.

## SOUL PRINCIPLE

*Only you can make the decisions and choices that affect and guide your life.*

—Dr. M. T. Morter, Jr.

**BOOSTER THOUGHT #2**
**Each new day is a new beginning**

Each day is a new beginning, a fresh start. Each day is the first day of the rest of your life. You've heard these maxims, yet have you ever really *experienced* one for yourself? Have you ever really *thought* of a new day in this manner?

Think about this: when you get up in the morning, you can make a new start. You can make changes in your life that will affect the rest of your days on this earth. Isn't that exciting? It is a marvelous feeling to know that the decisions I make today, *this* day, can mark the beginning of a new life for me. My life is determined according to the choices I make today. I can lie in bed all day eating donuts, drinking coffee, and watching TV—or I can hop up, go for a walk, eat some fruit, drink a glass of juice, and read an inspirational passage or two from a motivational source. I can dread my day at a dreary job or be thankful for the ability to work and better myself by learning from the experiences of the day. I can judge everyone and everything around me as stupid and unimportant or I can see others as unique and equal. I can strike out with anger or open my arms with love. It is my choice.

I can be sad, blue, depressed, and lonely or I can be happy, loving, accepting, and at peace. I can literally shape my way of thinking, acting, and being by choosing to do so. If it is to be, it is up to me. Happiness, which I equate with being at peace, being harmonious in soul and spirit, comes from within. Happiness cannot be given to you. You cannot take it from others. Your happiness is dependent upon *you*. You can get happy just like you got sad (or mad or grouchy or mean or whatever), all by yourself. That's right, you got yourself into the state you are in all by yourself.

You may say, "Oh, no I didn't. It was my husband who made me like this. He was so this or that all the time that I had to get like this to live with him." However, my point is that you allowed his being this or that to affect you the way it did. You let him cause you to be angry, sad, mean, or whatever. You chose to react the way you did. You could have chosen, and can still choose, to be happy. You can choose to let his actions just roll off of you, like water off a duck's back. You can choose to reach a spiritual plane in which you do not judge him or his actions and you do not let his actions shape your being. When you reach this state, you will love him more and expect less from him. Your happiness becomes just that, *yours*. It is up to you to choose to be happy and even if you may have blown it for today, make tomorrow count. When you get up in the morning, make it a happy day. Choose to be thankful for each day, learning from each experience, seeing the good in each experience, and being happy for the privilege to do so. Remember, you will be happier if you choose to be nice rather than right as you interact with and react to other people.

## SOUL PRINCIPLE

*Every day offers the opportunity to start anew.*
—Dr. M. T. Morter, Jr.

# Thoughts on Fear

### BOOSTER THOUGHT #1
### Living in fear

To live in fear is an unhealthy state of mind, as fear is one of the most powerful negative emotions, one that will actually rule your life if you let it. Fear separates you from the universal power. It causes a block in the flow of the spiritual energy within you. Allowing fear to control your consciousness guarantees that you will experience ill health in some form. Mental anguish may be the most obvious form, but deep-rooted fear is most likely the cause for many serious diseases.

Identifying or recognizing the fears in your life is the first step toward dealing with them. Many patients who attend my health retreats don't even realize, initially, that fear is the culprit behind their health problems. We fear so much and it is fear that causes many of our problems today. One of the most common fears I find when working with patients is a fear of losing or never attaining happiness.

Fear and other negative emotions cause the production of endorphins in your body and your body must respond. The response is often negative. According to animal experiments, some endorphins may cause the growth of tumors and impair learning or memory. Blair Justice, Ph.D., has conducted studies that have shown that "alpha-endorphin and other opioid peptides secreted under inescapable stress, suppress the function of T-cells in the immune system and reduce the effectiveness of NK (natural killer) cells."[17] Natural killer cells are key in protecting the body from development of cancer and viral infection.

There are also cases of people who are literally "frightened to death" by terrifying experiences that do not cause physical harm, but produce emotional shock or intense anxiety. J.M.T. Finney, a professor of surgery at Johns Hopkins, has publicly reported that he would not perform surgery on people who believe they will not live through it.[18] In addition, Theodore Miller, senior attending surgeon at Memorial Sloan-Kettering Cancer Center in New York, reported the following to the Society of Surgical Oncology:

> "After operating on several patients who expressed great apprehension and fear of death, only to have them die in spite of what appeared to be a normal operative course, I no longer operate on a patient who expresses the fear that he would not survive the operation."[19]

It seems that a person who is "scared to death" is literally just that. They may apparently "die from fright" by overstimulating the sympathetic nervous system and adrenal medulla. This leads to shock and blood pressure failure. Now I am not suggesting that everyone who lives in fear is going to die of shock. Far from it. But I am saying that a state of fear causes your body to respond physiologically. You have no choice; it is automatic.

However, you do have a choice in the emotional state in which you live. You may feel that your life is out of control and that you have no choice but to be afraid. I'm telling you that you do have a choice. You may need to reevaluate your conditions or situation. You may need to write down your options or list the

pros and cons in your life. Take a good look at your life and determine what changes or steps need to be made in order to rectify
your situation. Tackle one thing at a time. The best way to handle
your fears is to face them head-on.

What is it that you are *really* afraid of? Are you really afraid
about not being able to pay the rent? Or is it that you are not
secure in your overall financial status? Maybe instead of focusing
on getting the rent money, you need to focus on getting a job
that would eliminate the worry. Or maybe you need to get a place
that has a lower rent. Maybe you could get a roommate.

Are you *really* afraid that Mary is going to leave you? Or are
you insecure in your ability to live alone? Or is it that you're
afraid of what others would think about it (again, insecurity)?
Maybe you need to build your self-esteem. You could read books,
take a course, or develop your faith in prayer and open yourself
up to the universal spirit to gain strength.

The point is to evaluate the fearful situations in your life.
Determine what your true fears are and take action steps to eliminate these fears. Finding and addressing your fears will have an
incredibly positive impact on your life. You may find that seeking
professional help is necessary. Many people turn to their minis-
ters, seek counsel from psychiatrists or psychologists, or rely on
the support of good friends or family when they are attempting
to overcome obstacles in their lives. Many patients who attend
my health retreats are looking for help with emotional conditions as well as physical ailments. All of this seems to work, but I
also strongly recommend seeking your own counsel.

At my health retreats, I teach people to listen to their inner
powers, to let go with their conscious minds and turn on to their
subconscious energies. They learn that they are in control of their
lives and that they are responsible for their health. It's all about
you. You have the power; you have the universal energy within
you. When you know this, your fears may be abandoned. You will
have the patience to allow the power to work. You will be able to
give up your fears and depend on your faith as you enter the new
state of knowingness.

# SOUL PRINCIPLE

*Fear separates you from the universal power.*
—Dr. M. T. Morter, Jr.

## BOOSTER THOUGHT #2
### Seeing the big picture

Franklin Roosevelt was so right when he said, "The only thing we have to fear is fear itself." The very act of fearing is one that causes despair. Fear comes wrapped in a variety of packages: worry, dread, loneliness, and hopelessness to name a few. If you study the root feeling behind many negative emotions, you will find that the base is fear. Fear is the common denominator in many of our greatest challenges. It solicits anxiety and rattles our confidence. It encircles us with a feeling of impending doom. It's just downright scary.

So, what do we do? How do we handle it? I believe that the best way to handle our fears is to tackle them. If we don't, then we are destined for failure. Fear *insures* failure. Where there is fear, there is doubt, and that combination is self-defeating. Just an inkling of either emotion blocks the spiritual energy within you. If you live in fear, you cannot be experiencing the true flow of God's spiritual power. It is not possible to know fear and know that you are one with the universal energy at the same time. This is a dichotomy that is impossible.

In order to overcome your fears, you must see them for what they are. Fears are only minute specks of your imagination within the greater expanse of universal energy and power. Confront your fears and deal with them one at a time or, better yet, turn them over to the power that is within you. Open your mind and soul to the true healing force that is the creator of all. Believe and know that you can and will rise above your fears, that you can turn your failures into lessons for success in the future. Meditate and be thankful for the positive things that you wish to manifest in your life—love, peace, security, confidence, or whatever. You can believe these attributes to be a part of your life even before they are fully developed. As you begin to feel at peace and confident, then you will find that fear no longer resides within you.

Fear is disharmonious with the spiritual energies. Karol Truman writes in her book, *Feelings Buried Alive Never Die,* that "**FEAR** is the dark room where all the negatives are developed."[20] How true that is. Where there is true peace and harmony, there is not fear. Just as mosquitos cannot live in a body of water that is flowing freely, fear cannot reside in you if the energy of your soul and spirit are flowing freely. To rise above the disquiet of fear, you must see the big picture of the universe. You can choose to live as a harmonious contributor to the universal intelligence, allowing the energy to flow through you—not as an inhibited block of dammed-up energy. When you understand and are fully "in-the-know," you will see yourself as an integral, if small, part of the big picture.

I am not making light of your feelings, such as fear, when I simply say to overcome them. Having worked in the health profession for many years, I realize it may take some time to deal with deep-rooted emotions. Every month, patients come to my health retreats who have been living in fear, anger, or the like for many years. They have even tried, unsuccessfully, to deal with it. It is only through truly identifying, then confronting, these emotions (and the catalyst that spurred them in the first place) that they are successful. Remember that there may be many branches to your emotions. By some similarity or connotation, an early fear may trigger a new fear today. The key is to work through fears one at a time, keeping in mind that positive, loving thoughts poured onto your fears will wash them away. See the lesson your fears present you with, learn that lesson, and put it behind you. By doing so you are freeing the energy of your soul to flow fluidly with the true spiritual energy within you.

## SOUL PRINCIPLE

*Where there is peace and harmony, there is no fear.*
—Dr. M. T. Morter, Jr.

# Thoughts on Judgment

### BOOSTER THOUGHT #1
### Judge not

It is easier to say, "Judge not, lest ye be judged" than it is to practice the precept. Keep in mind that nothing is good or bad, right or wrong, until you judge it so, and then it is merely your perception. That is all that judgment really is—one's perception of a given event, person, action, or thing. Shakespeare wrote of the qualities of man's character in *Hamlet*. Among other very good advice, he warned to "reserve thy judgment."

One of the greatest ironies of judgment is that, when we are judging we think we are performing positive thinking because we are sure that our judgment is *right*. However, I believe the mere act of judging is a negative one. To judge is to rate something using your opinion as the scale. Sometimes your opinion is based on certain theologies, philosophies, or doctrines that have been handed down for generations, but that does not change the basis for your judgment, which remains *your opinion*. It also doesn't matter that your opinion may be one that is held by others, perhaps many others. We judge when we want others to learn *our* lessons.

The fact is, judging—whether judging others, their actions, events, or anything else—is a process of rating according to your opinion and perception. Who are we to judge? Are we in such high esteem that we hold such a station in this universe that we should be able to judge? Isn't the act of judging one that affords us a self-appointed righteousness? Can we really sit back and believe that we have the right, that we are in a position, to judge? Our perceptions change over the course of our lifetimes—from childhood to teenage to adulthood to elderly—so, at what age do we judge rightly?

I believe that man has been given the power to think freely and that we often abuse this privilege by performing such acts as judgment with our minds. It is a difficult trait to overcome, a hard habit to break if it has become commonplace in one's life. However, I know that when a higher level of consciousness is attained, when you become in tune in soul and spirit, then the need or urge to judge dissipates. It becomes no longer necessary. It will no longer be a part of your life or your way of thinking.

When you reach this state of consciousness you will be overcome with a sense of loving and accepting. This feeling will wash over your being and affect your every waking moment. You will not need to judge others. You will actually love them more and expect less from them. Your ability to give unconditional love will be automatic. You will be living a life of peace, one of harmonious resonance with spirit and soul. Judgment will not be a part of that state of being.

So, as you go through your daily life, think about this:

> "A flippant, frivolous man may ridicule others, may controvert them, scorn them; but he who has any respect for himself seems to have renounced the right of thinking meanly of others."
>
> —Johann Wolfgang von Goethe

## SOUL PRINCIPLE

> Judgment is merely one's perception of a given person, event, action, or thing.
>
> —Dr. M. T. Morter, Jr.

**BOOSTER THOUGHT #2**
**The birthday present**

He first noticed that one of his garden statues was missing when he went for a walk on his grounds. While strolling through his gardens he looked over at one of his favorite spots only to find that his statue of St. Fiacre was missing. St. Fiacre, patron saint of gardeners, was a skilled horticulturist and a source of healing miracles. He loved his statue very much and spent valuable time sitting on the bench next to it; this was his meditation spot. Now his beloved statue was gone. He approached his revered spot, the one place on his property that he felt warranted the placement of St. Fiacre. Nothing else seemed to have been disturbed. Leaning down, he touched the place on the ground where St. Fiacre had stood.

Hurriedly, and with mounting concern, he began to search for the missing saint. Where on earth could it be? He looked behind the mounded flower bed, around the trees in the area, under the bench, and even in the koi pool. There was no sign of the missing statue. As he was frantically searching the area, a neighbor happened to be walking by and could see him. The neighbor called out to ask if he could be of assistance. The man walked over to his neighbor and told him about his predicament. Together the two performed a most thorough search of the area, but to no avail; they were unable to locate St. Fiacre. Thanking the neighbor for his time, the man sent him on his way.

He then walked back to his house, sat on his deck, and placed his head in his hands. It was in this state that his wife found him. Thinking the worst, she rushed to his side to ask what was the matter. Again, he told the story of the missing saint. The wife could not account for the loss, but wanted to see the now-somewhat-barren garden spot formerly occupied by St. Fiacre. So, with a long face and slumped shoulders, he led her to the site.

It was at this time that they saw a little boy, dressed in gardener's attire, walking down the lane pushing a miniature wheelbarrow. His little garden clogs flopped rhythmically as he moved along. They recognized the boy as a relatively new neighbor whom they didn't really know. As he got closer the man could see something in the boy's wheelbarrow. Upon closer inspection, he recognized that "something" as his precious statue of St. Fiacre.

The man's immediate reaction was one of anger. He called out for the boy to stop and he quickly ran to the little boy. The lecture he gave on the sacrilegious nature of stealing would have made his minister proud. He explained that to rob someone of their belongings was wrong—a great sin, in fact. In a righteous tone, he went on to tell the little boy that he would be reporting his felonious behavior to his parents. But he didn't stop there! His tirade pointed out that the little boy was "bad" and should be punished for stealing the statue. Eventually, his steam began to run down, and he asked the little boy if he had anything to say for himself.

Looking up at the man, with innocent, clear green eyes that overflowed with tears, the little boy said, "It's not what you think, Mr. Jones. You see, since we moved next door to you I have watched you working in your garden. I really liked to watch you in the spot where this guy stood, because he seemed to make you happy. You would just sit on that bench and talk to him. I wanted to be like you, so when you were inside I would go to that bench and talk to him, too. I told him about my birthday and I told him that I wanted to be like you. And I told him that I wanted a wheelbarrow and gardener's clothes for my birthday. Then I told him that if I got them, I would take him to meet my mom. See, she has cancer and can't get out of bed anymore. I was just bringing him back."

You see, the little boy was not a "bad" boy, nor did he need to be punished. It was simply the man's perception and judgment that clouded the real issue. The man had jumped to form an opinion, a judgment, of the situation and the boy. As it is with other people and situations, our judgment or perception of them may be lacking in fundamental issues of importance. When we don't know the whole picture, we can't begin to understand the workings behind other's actions. How much do we really know about life that would allow us to judge?

## SOUL PRINCIPLE

*Nothing is good or bad, until judgement names it so.*
—Dr. M. T. Morter, Jr.

# Thoughts on Love

### BOOSTER THOUGHT #1
### Love is the way

When I think about love, I also think about the spirit. They are one and the same to me. It is impossible to separate spirit (God) and love. It is the unconditional love of the awesome universal spirit that created all. In the eyes of the spirit, everything is loved, perfect, and whole. Our goal to become one with the spirit requires that we begin to see through those same, non-judging eyes. It requires that we emit love, think loving thoughts, and fill our spiritual fields with love.

## SOUL PRINCIPLE

*It is my firm belief that it is love that sustains the earth. There only is life where there is love. Life without love is death. Love is the reverse of the coin of which the obverse is Truth.*

—Mahatma Gandhi

The more we love, the more we grow and attain in all areas of our lives. Truly loving, *unconditionally*, creates a sense of peacefulness and harmony that not only allows for, but actually demands, oneness in soul and spirit. In order to practice this, you must eradicate feelings of fear, hate, jealousy, and judgment from your life. These negative emotions block your freedom to experience unconditional love. As long as you allow such negativity in your thoughts, you will not be able to attain the oneness I am talking about.

To remove these negative feelings from your life, quickly "cancel" them whenever they pop into your head. Simply think or say aloud, "I cancel that thought." Then replace it with a loving, unconditional thought—a thought that envelops with love the person or experience that elicited it. Loving in this manner will take you one step closer to the spiritual path. Sometimes it is even necessary to read an inspirational passage from a favorite book. The stories in the *Chicken Soup for the Soul* series of books serve as great sources of inspiration. Mark Victor Hansen and Jack Canfield do a marvelous job of compiling "shining examples of the best qualities we all share as human beings: compassion, grace, forgiveness, hope, courage, dedication, generosity, and faith."[21] We must take an action step toward creating harmony within. In fact, it is only by establishing oneness with your soul and your spirit that you can ascend to the highest level of your consciousness. Continuing to judge, hate, fear, and such actually creates a separation between your soul and your spirit.

God's love for you is without bounds and unconditional in nature. It is not restricted or governed. It is the free will that God bestowed upon you that allows you to either love unconditionally or to judge and hate. In Corinthians 13 it is written that "love is patient, love is kind. It does not envy, it does not boast, it is not proud. It is not rude, it is not self-seeking, it is not easily angered, it keeps no record of wrongs. Love does not delight in evil but rejoices with the truth. It always protects, always trusts, always hopes, always perseveres. Love never fails."

If you choose to love as God loves you, unconditionally, then you will live in oneness. However, if you restrict your love with judgment, hate, fear, jealousy, and other negative feelings, or withhold it altogether, then your conditional love will keep you separated in soul and spirit. As these negative emotions block your ability to achieve oneness, they also put negativity into your field, thus attracting negativity to you.

You cause a conflict, imbalance, or blockage when you use your free will to perform acts of judgment, hatred, and the like. This conflict within you will manifest itself in illness and, as I have said before, the illness, condition, or disease will vary from person to person. However, it is certain that some form of ill health will be created if you do not love in God's way. The power of love can and will attract to you all of the good things you desire— loving relationships, professional success, health, or anything else.

There is an immense and calming freedom that comes with loving unconditionally. At this point in your development you will no longer feel the need to judge others or their actions. You will no longer feel the pangs of jealousy or the fires of hatred burning within you. You won't be chained to fear or lost in loneliness. Once you can unconditionally love others and the world around you, you are freed of all those negative feelings. They will no longer exist in your soul or interfere with your perfect spiritual plane. You will have pulled them up by the roots and done away with them. A calm, peaceful existence, free of negativity, full of positive, loving thoughts is the way of God. Love is the way of God. Make it your way.

# SOUL PRINCIPLE

*Unconditional love creates peace, harmony, and oneness in soul and spirit.*

—Dr. M. T. Morter, Jr.

**BOOSTER THOUGHT #2**
**Peace in loving**

In the grand scheme of things, unconditional love is the greatest gift one can give or receive. The mere act of loving creates a feeling of peace and fulfillment within us. It is a joyous emotion and one that is necessary and vital to your existence. History has shown that children raised in environments in which they did not receive love, grew to be cold, angry, and often violent adults. The lack of love can cause extreme loneliness, anger, or other negative emotions. These negative feelings, left to grow internally, will manifest in disease or ill health.

Love, on the other hand, creates a sense of peace, which encompasses confidence, freedom, and joy. Unconditional love, given and received, promotes good health and harmony in soul and spirit. True peace is an all-encompassing experience brought on by unconditional love; peace is made known to you by your mind. Physical pleasures may elicit peace, as well as spiritual endeavors. However the feeling of peace is one that is made apparent by your mind. It is with your mind that you consciously know peacefulness.

Love is the thread that binds peacefulness to your being. To reach a state of peace you must achieve a balance or alignment in the three planes of your existence—physical, mental, and spiritual. The body, mind, or spirit alone cannot give you peace. Peace and healing result when there is a harmonious balance between your soul (mind and body) and your spirit (God). Unconditional love is the source of peace. It is by loving more and expecting less that you can reach this state of peaceful harmony.

Here are some tips for reaching a state of peace through unconditional love.

- Each time you perform an act of love you feed your spiritual field with positive energy. This serves to heal the soul. Make it a part of your life to do something loving for yourself and someone else every single day. This will help to balance your energy and remove blockage within your body.
- Keep in mind that every negative thought or feeling needs to be "canceled" or neutralized. To do this, replace the negative emotion with a positive feeling of unconditional love. Your love needs to be as strong as your negative feeling in order for this to work.
- Work to attain oneness in soul and spirit by practicing unconditional love. Remember, each act of judgment, hate, anger, etc. serves to create separateness. As long as you feel separated from God, you block the energy that works to allow you to walk as one with God.
- Set aside some quiet time each day to meditate on your life, your intentions, and your thoughts. Consider each area of your life and draw conclusions that will help to bring your soul and spirit together as one. Reflect on how you can change aspects of your life by filling your days with unconditional love.
- Surrender your egotistical mind to God's power or energy—the unconditional love and universal energy that is within you. Allow your challenges and pursuits to be given over to this innate spiritual energy. Practice unconditional love and have faith in this powerful force that is you.
- Give thanks in prayer for your ability to give and receive unconditional love. Be aware of the many facets of your life that are touched by the showing of this love.
- Keep in mind that you do not have to love the personality or the actions of everyone. What you need to love is the spirit within them, even if they have

let their egotistical self block the perfect flow or display of that spirit. Love them as your equal in God's creation. Love them because you share the universal consciousness and almighty spirit with them. All men and women are created equally, spiritually.

- Thinking one way and acting another creates disharmony between your soul and your spirit. Be true and congruent within yourself. Your thoughts and actions need to agree. In other words, practice what you preach (even to yourself).

Recognizing the power of unconditional love is an awe-inspiring event. If you have ever witnessed the care of a parent for a dying child, the acts of a child toward an ailing parent, or the love of one spouse for another in a grave situation then you have most likely been touched by the manifestation of unconditional love. As a physician, I have been privy to the demonstration of unconditional love many times over the years. I never cease to be touched and positively affected by it.

Align yourself with the spiritual path by expressing unconditional love. Strive to overcome negative emotions by smothering them with this love, and know that you are becoming one with the divine, universal source of energy that many of us call God when you give and receive unconditional love. Putting love into your field will attract positive and loving people, things, and acts to you. As you give, so shall you receive. You can attain a state of peace by thinking and acting with unconditional love as your cornerstone.

## SOUL PRINCIPLE

*Unconditional love is the greatest gift one can give or receive.*

—Dr. M. T. Morter, Jr.

## BOOSTER THOUGHT #3
### Enough love

My daughter-in-law related this story to me about thirteen years ago when her second child was born. It seems appropriate to share it with you now.

Since she was a girl, she had always looked forward to the time when she would be a mother. A true lover of children, she even completed bachelor's and master's degrees in elementary education. Teaching school in several different states and types of school districts, she found that each school had its own set of challenges and assets, but the children were her motivating factor. After marrying my son in 1983, she moved to the city where he was living to start their life together.

To our delight, she became pregnant within a few months. Wanting to raise their family in a small town, they decided to leave the city. They had each grown up in small towns about thirty miles apart. This was home to them and they each still had family in that area. It was important to them to have their children grow up near grandparents, aunts, uncles, and cousins. Shortly after the move (about one week later) our beautiful baby granddaughter was born. My son said they unpacked everything that week!

As my daughter-in-law relates this story she describes an unconditional love that is almost overwhelming to her. Here is the letter that she wrote to baby Sarah the week that she was born.

*My dearest Sarah,*

*Hello, baby. I've waited so long to see you and hold you in my arms. Since I was little girl I've loved babies and dreamed of one day having my own. Now, finally, that day has come.*

*These last nine months have held some of the most special times of my life. I'll never forget feeling you move inside of me for the first time and then feeling the movements growing stronger with time. I can't describe to you how that made me feel. (Wonderful. Awesome. Exciting. So very happy. Those words can't come close, but they'll have to suffice.)*

*I felt so close to you even before you were born.
Now that you're here I feel so proud and happy to have
you as my daughter. You make my life complete, little
girl. I love you so much, Sarah.*
*Mommy*

Now baby Sarah had grown to be a much-loved toddler when our daughter-in-law found out that she was pregnant again. Oh, what a happy time it was for all of us. We were all anxiously awaiting the birth of their second child. My daughter-in-law very much wanted another baby and was extremely healthy throughout the pregnancy. It was only toward the end that she admitted to herself a nagging doubt—a doubt that continued to haunt her.

She feared that she could not love another child as much as she loved Sarah. Sarah had come to *represent* love to her. She felt such a strong maternal bond to the little girl that she was afraid that she wouldn't be able to love the new baby with the same intensity. This fear was never made public knowledge, it was never spoken, but it was very real to her for the last few days of the pregnancy. She said she would try to convince herself that it wouldn't be that way when the baby was born, but she still had a little doubt right up to the moment that he was born.

Not surprisingly, her worries and fears completely dissipated the moment she laid eyes on baby Russell. The very instant that she saw him she knew that her love for him wholeheartedly matched her love for Sarah. I was in the birthing room and witnessed for myself the feeling of love that washed over the mother, father, and new baby. It was immediate and quite obvious. In fact, she says she knew then that she could have an unlimited number of babies and there would not only be enough love, there would be *more* than enough love. The love she felt for Sarah actually grew to encompass the new baby and she knew it would continue to grow forever. This is the way with unconditional love.

## SOUL PRINCIPLE

*Unconditional love grows and encompasses more, forever.*
—Dr. M. T. Morter, Jr.

# Thoughts on Forgiveness

## BOOSTER THOUGHT #1
### The steps of forgiveness

As was discussed in Chapter 2, subconscious emotional memory override often runs our physical bodies. These stored memory patterns elicit negative responses, leading us to ill health and, often, disease. In order to neutralize a negative subconscious memory or emotion, I offer you the steps of forgiveness. True forgiveness of negative experiences you have lived through and with can actually change your state of health. These forgiveness steps are quite simple in concept, but keep in mind they must be carried out with feeling and emotion. If you are not sincere, then you are wasting your time and energy.

Before you perform the steps of forgiveness, you must do a little self-actualization work. To become more aware of what is affecting your life, do this memory update: 1) Identify a situation, action, or person that you feel needs to be forgiven. Think of something from your past that you did not like or that you wish had turned out differently. What you identify may have occurred at any time in your life—yesterday, last week, last year, or when you were six years old. (A person held in esteem or great affection is often identified.) 2) Acknowledge that this incident did, in fact, occur. Think about the situation, recalling your feelings, thoughts, and emotions on the subject. 3) Realize that trying to forget such events actually just places them in the subconscious where they fester, finally causing ill health.

Having identified and thought about a person, action, or situation, you are now ready to begin the steps of forgiveness. *Remember, you do not have to agree with the actions of the other person or the event in order to forgive. You are forgiving for your own sake, not someone else's. Until you forgive the past, this other person or event is controlling your life. This is true even if the other person is now dead!* In addition, when you truly forgive you give up the urge to "get even"; you will no longer feel the need for revenge. You will actually be thankful that this event occurred in your life. You will see the good in it. If you follow the

steps, with sincerity of heart, you are on the way to enlightenment, as well as to improved health. You can do it!

1.  *Self forgiveness*. You must first forgive yourself for
    allowing the event to affect your health. Forgive
    yourself for any harm you may have caused your-
    self because of this situation, action, or person.
    Literally say, "I forgive myself for any harm I may
    have caused myself because of (whomever)."
2.  *Forgive the other person*. Next, you must forgive
    the other person for any harm he or she may have
    caused you. Again, literally say these words, "I for-
    give (whomever) for any harm he or she may have
    caused me."
3.  *Give the other person permission to forgive you*.
    It is not necessary, or even recommended, that the
    other person know that you are taking this step. It
    is, in fact, immaterial. It doesn't matter whether
    they know or not, because you are doing this for
    *you*, not for him or her. The other person may even
    be deceased and that's okay, too. The forgiveness
    takes place within *you*. You now say, "I give (whom-
    ever) absolute permission to forgive me for any
    harm I may have caused him or her."

The vital key to the steps of forgiveness is *sincerity*. In order
for these steps to affect you and your health, you must perform
them with feeling and emotion. You have to mean it when you
say the words. You may be thinking, "How can I possibly forgive
Uncle Joe for raping me?" Or maybe your situation is the time
you got slapped in the face for something you didn't do. Or perhaps your mother beat you every day of your young life. Or maybe
you yell at your kids. Or ... anything.

In my clinical experience, I have encountered many traumatic situations with a myriad of patients over the years. It is not
necessary to agree with the person or the event, but it *is* imperative to your health that you forgive it. Not only must you forgive
it, you must actually learn to see the good in it. Learn the lessons

that it brought into your life. Why is it good that this happened to you? What did you or can you learn from it? It may be that the best thing you can think of is that you would never do this to someone else. Or maybe you learned exactly how *not* to treat another person or child. Maybe you learned that you can help others who experience similar treatment. The point is, learn from the situation. Learn the lesson that life (maybe literally) slapped you with and see the good in it. It is in the past, understand how you are better because of it.

Nothing ever happens *to* you, it happens *for* you to learn a lesson. If the lesson is learned correctly and well, it will better enable you to give and receive unconditional love. Be thankful for the lesson of the moment. If you can learn the lesson as it is presented, you don't have to store it in memory and let it fester until it reveals itself as some disease, headache, pain, or ailment.

Rather than trying to forget an unhappy or stressful event, make it a loving, learning, living experience. Blanket it with love, enlightenment, and understanding. As the lesson is learned and you truly believe that you are a better person because of it, you will be able to cover it with unconditional love. Then the interference it has caused between you and the perfect spiritual energy will be diminished. You will take a giant step toward the spiritual path. You will begin to resonate more harmoniously in soul and spirit.

## SOUL PRINCIPLE

*Apply the steps of forgiveness to the lesson of the moment,*
*seeing the good in each situation.*

—Dr. M. T. Morter, Jr.

**BOOSTER THOUGHT #2**
**What a headache!**

This is a story about a patient, Sally, who came to me complaining of migraine headaches. Sally, who is about forty years old, stated that she has had a migraine headache every day for the past twenty years. Not occasionally, not once a week, but *every* day. She said, "Dr. Morter, no matter what I do, I develop a headache at some point during the day, every day. Medication sometimes dulls the pain, but the headaches *never* go away completely." She said they hurt; they pounded so hard that she sometimes thought that the pain would kill her.

She discovered, through self-evaluation, that her migraine headaches had actually started the day she got a divorce. She also realized that she had never forgiven her husband for leaving her for another woman. As a result, she had a migraine headache every day since their divorce.

I asked Sally to think about the frequency with which she thought of her ex-husband. How often did she actually think about him? Sally said to me, "Well, Doc, I think about him every day. In fact, often I think of him more than once per day." This realization helped Sally become aware that her feelings of hate toward her husband were affecting her daily life. She then became aware that these negative emotions were actually causing her physical pain. Once she made that connection, she said it was like a light switch had been turned on. She was then able to forgive him— for her own sake, not his.

This doesn't mean that she approved of what he did. It means that she forgave him for his actions, which freed her of her headaches. And they have never returned. I spoke with her recently and she is still in awe of the power of forgiveness. She practices the steps of forgiveness on a daily basis, not only in the case of her ex-husband, but also as they apply to other issues in her life.

Sally was a chained slave to her ex-husband and her divorce. He had been in control of her life every day for the past twenty years and she didn't even know it. While he was happy and remarried with two children, she was miserable every day. She was not affecting his life by hating him, but she was destroying her own. Sally decided to take charge of her life, which resulted in being pain free. She forgave her ex to save herself. Her forgiveness probably had no more affect on him than did her hate. It was done for her own good, not his. And it worked! It can work for you, too. Is there a thought or experience that comes into your mind often? Is it from the past? You may find these steps of forgiveness will work wonders in *your* life.

## SOUL PRINCIPLE

*Forgiving is for you, not for anyone else.*
—Dr. M. T. Morter, Jr.

# Thoughts on Indecision

**BOOSTER THOUGHT #1**
**To marry or not to marry?**

There was a thirty year old man who ran a dairy farm with his father. He milked forty cows per day, every day. It was a regular part of his life. One day, after he performed his daily chores, which included milking the cows, he fell into bed, exhausted. The next morning he awoke to find that he could not get out of bed. He had no pain; he just couldn't get up. He was too weak. When his stomach began to churn he finally forced himself to get out of bed to go to the bathroom. Then he found that he not only had diarrhea, but blood in the stool. At this point, he came to see me.

Upon hearing his story, I immediately realized that he had had some type of mental anguish recently. I knew that these symptoms were often found in old age and the occurrence of these symptoms in such a young person led me to know that they were related to certain strong feelings. Most frequently, I find that diarrhea and blood in the stool are related to worry, indecision, or a similar feeling. Typically, a specific event produces such acute complaints.

I asked him what had been on his mind, if he was worried about something. He related that he had divorced a few years back. His wife had received half of his cattle in the divorce settlement, which was forty cows. That was a huge loss to him. He then said that he had been really lonely since his divorce. The funny thing about it all, he said, was that now he had found someone new to share his life. He felt that he should be happy, but instead he was worried. He was to get married the next Saturday, but all he could think about was what would happen if they divorced and she took half of his cows. He wouldn't have the money to keep his farm running. He wouldn't be able to help his elderly parents. He would be financially devastated. He said he was in a real conflict between remaining lonely or marrying and perhaps losing everything. He couldn't decide what to do, so he just kept worrying about it. It had now gotten so bad that he couldn't even get out of bed.

I explained to him that this was the solution his body had worked out for him. He had solved his problem at a subconscious level. If he couldn't get out of bed, he couldn't get married, couldn't get divorced, and couldn't lose his farm. He had solved his problem without the use of his conscious mind. He created this solution with his indecision and worry.

In my office, I worked with him to balance his body. Using the technique I have developed, I removed the interference in his energy by reversing the process he had used to cause the interference in the first place. In this book, I aim to teach you how to reverse the steps you took to get to your current state. If you are sick, depressed, or in some negative state of health and *want* to improve, you can. Then you will need to take the time to identify the events in your life that caused your emotional stress. You will find that acute occurrences of emotional upheaval brought on certain health conditions. The technique that I have developed over the past thirty-nine years, and use in my office treatments, helps people to identify sources of problems and overcome their challenges in order to eliminate them. There is help available to anyone who wants help. That help begins with you, but you may need a trained healthcare practitioner to guide you on your journey to regain your health.

The result of our session was that this man was fine within twenty-four hours of the onset of his problems. The diarrhea and bleeding subsided just as quickly as they had developed. He recognized that his indecision had caused his physical condition. He faced his worries and married the next Saturday.

There was another healthcare option that this man could have taken. He could have treated his diarrhea with medication. In doing so, he would have been treating his problem from the outside, by putting a foreign substance into the body. His body would have then been forced to respond to these chemicals. They might have stopped his diarrhea for the time being, but they would not have gotten to the cause of the diarrhea. In addition, his body would have then been stressed by having to respond to the medication. Medication attacks the physical problem, but the physical problem is only an effect of the cause that is in the mental plane.

Become aware of the cause of your health conditions. The symptoms and ailments expressed in the physical plane have their roots in the mental, emotional plane. Furthermore, these physical symptoms come about unknowingly. In other words, you don't consciously create them; they are created at the subconscious level as reactions to your mental state. They become a reality because of your mental focus or concentration—your negative feelings and emotions. The body is aware of the chemical production caused by negative emotion. It reacts and becomes exhausted. The exhaustion may be of a particular organ or an entire system. It may express itself as a cold, the flu, diarrhea, fibromyalgia, chronic fatigue, or general malaise.

I'm not saying, "It's all in your head." I acknowledge that there is pain and that it is very real. Any pain or disease is a perfect response by a perfect system to the energy of the soul. When the soul's energy is negative, the expression in the physical plane is disease. To reverse the disease process one must improve the energy of the soul. To do this will take some effort. We have to change the way we think, the way we respond to events in our lives, the way we respond to others and their actions, and the way we view our role on earth. We must be aware that what we think about, we bring about. "As a man thinketh, so is he" are not mere words, but a basic spiritual premise that serves to guide humanity. What we believe is what we bring into our lives.

## SOUL PRINCIPLE

*Physical symptoms are created at the subconscious level as reactions to your mental state.*

—Dr. M. T. Morter, Jr.

**BOOSTER THOUGHT #2**
**What is beyond belief?**

As is discussed in the last chapter, there is a state of being beyond belief, a place where there is no room for indecision, judgment, anger, or the like. It is a place where total peace and harmony preside. In this place, fulfillment comes in "knowing." Furthermore, this "knowingness" is an inner state that exists within each of us, although not everyone opens the door to this sanctum. Carl Jung, in his book *Modern Man in Search of a Soul*, outlined the developmental stages of adulthood. In his book he describes each of the stages and explains the progression of moving from one stage to the next. He states that people may become fixated in one of the stages and never proceed in development past that stage. The last stage of adult development he calls the spirit. He characterizes the spirit stage as an awareness that the earth is not our home, that we were made up of energy that is constantly changing. Furthermore, he states that the energy that is within us is infinite, celestial, universal, and eternal in nature— and only temporary within this physical body.[22]

I suggest that these stages may not be reserved for adulthood, but may begin in the younger, formative years. I have encountered many young people who, especially in the final throes of an illness, have reached the higher levels of personal development—Jung's spirit stage. I am in agreement with Dr. Jung in several areas of his work. Jung believed in a collective unconscious. This is the same as what I call the universal consciousness. According to Jung, the collective unconscious included archetypes, which are thought patterns that have developed through the centuries. Jung believed that archetypes enabled people to react to situations in ways similar to the way their ancestors reacted. He further believed that the collective unconscious contained wisdom that served to guide all of humanity. He even believed that archetypes of gods and supernatural powers were contained in the collective unconscious.

It is exciting to me each time I find resources that further confirm and substantiate my philosophical and clinical findings. Each of these experiences assures me that there is only one truth, one source, and one path. In the beginning, there was "the Word" and today the word still reigns. Indecision about this will only lead to discomfort, disharmony, and disease. While not everyone wants to reach the state of higher development or consciousness, it does exist and is available to each person.

While many people believe in God, there is a state beyond belief. This state or level of development concerns knowing. I don't mean knowing *about* God, but knowing God (or whatever you call the divine power). It is a state of being in direct communion and communication with your spiritual force. To know, to truly know, leaves no room for doubt or indecision, but moves past all negative emotions to a higher spiritual awareness. When you reach this heightened state of being, you will know it. You will no longer feel the tugs of judgment, worry, hate, indecision, or such. Those harsh negative emotions will be smothered by positive spiritual assuredness. There will be no room for self-seeking, but only for admittance to the spiritual truths. You will be enveloped in a sense of acceptance and unconditional love, living in a peaceful world where harmony of soul and spirit reign.

To reach this state beyond belief you must first acknowledge its existence. Then, you must consciously work to make contact with your spiritual force. There are a variety of ways to reach this higher level of consciousness. You may take steps toward this spiritual harmony through prayer, with conscious thought, by your actions, or through the use of meditation. You may not succeed in approaching every situation the way you know your spiritual being would. That's okay, keep at it. As long as it is your intention to achieve spiritual harmony and you work toward it constantly, then you will succeed. The spiritual energy is always ready and waiting to be utilized. At some point you will realize that you have reached this higher level of consciousness, that your thoughts, actions, and daily life portray it. You will eventually find that you automatically react with unconditional love, instead of with judgment or anger.

Keep in mind that the relationship between your soul and the spirit is unique. It is not in a collective group that you will find this inner sanctum, but via your personal endeavors. It's between you and God. No one else is a part of or needs to be privy to your private relationship with God. Colossians 3:11 says, *"Christ is all, and in all."* Knowing this, move upward in your development and strive to reach the higher level of consciousness that resides within you. I assure you, it is beyond belief.

## SOUL PRINCIPLE

*Beyond belief is a state of knowingness that moves one to a higher spiritual awareness.*

—Dr. M. T. Morter, Jr.

# Thoughts on Beliefs and Attitudes

### BOOSTER THOUGHT #1
### What does it mean to say, "It's God's will"?

We think we have many choices in free will. As I see it, we all must make one *primary* choice and we must truly *believe* in this choice. One option is to believe in a power that is greater than you—God, Allah, Buddha, the King, Ohm, *prana*, chi, life force, odic force, innate intelligence, or whatever else you might deem to call it. In addition, you must believe that this power is perfect, all-knowing, omnipotent, and omniscient. And furthermore, that everything is in existence because of this power. The other option is *not* to believe in this power. I have lived my life in a state of belief in God. I know that he exists and is the ultimate source of energy and power.

In my opinion, there is no doubt about God's will. His will is perfect. It is simply a master plan that *is*. There is no reasoning, judgment, or thinking on God's part. There is but one way, his way, the perfect way.

I do not believe it is ever God's will for someone to be sick. I had a young woman at a health retreat recently who was very ill. As the mother of five, she was quite concerned about her health, since she was unable to care for her children. Her ailment had been diagnosed as chronic fatigue syndrome. She simply had no energy. This young woman had been to many doctors and clinics prior to arriving at my health retreat. She had been through lengthy fasts and other forms of treatment in an attempt to heal her condition. Nothing had worked to date. She couldn't even get out of bed most days. After talking with her for a only few minutes, I recognized that she was a deeply religious person. She told me she was worried about the fact that she had not been able to attend church for several years; she prayed many times a day about her condition.

I asked her to share with the group exactly what and how she prayed. Her prayer went something like this: "God, please don't make me be so tired. If it is your will, I'd like to feel better." Group discussion followed in which it was pointed out that changing one word in her prayer would make it better. Changing "if" to "since" would create the perfect prayer. "Dear God, *since* it is your will, I'd like to feel better." What a difference one word makes! I'm proud to say that this young woman experienced what she termed a "miracle" that week. In fact, she told me later that changing just that one word and understanding the truth about God's will had a profound effect on her outlook and her health. Of course, her illness was much more involved than the changing of a word, but she learned that week how to deal with her illness, to get to the *cause* of her condition.

You see, it is God's will that we are all healthy and live happy, successful lives. He is not a punishing, vindictive God. Too often man has used the phrase "It's God's will" as an excuse, under the pretense of religion. "It's okay for me to be miserable, poor, sick, or whatever, because I prayed to God to change things for me and he didn't; therefore it's his will that I'm this way." Under these circumstances you have failed to realize that you have done nothing to change your own situation. Simply praying to God, but making no effort to correct or change things on your part, doesn't imply that it is God's will, but that it is *your* will. You make the choices that lead to the condition you are in; therefore, it is your will to be the way you are. The only way to change your situation is to change your life, by changing your lifestyle, your thoughts, and your actions.

If you have a disease or condition that you don't really like, then you must acknowledge that you have continued to do all the things that make your disease or condition necessary. Praying for God to cure you or your state of being will not change things for you. Understand that God didn't create your disease, so he won't cure your disease. He gave *you* the ability and responsibility to cure yourself. That's why the more drugs you take and the more surgery you have, the less likely you are to be healthy. Think about this: How many parts have to be cut out of a sick person to end up with a healthy whole?

You must take charge of your life by reaching a higher level of consciousness. Open your heart and your mind to the fact that you have the power within you to change your current conditions, to live a happy, healthy, productive, and successful life. If you are under the care of a physician, I do not suggest that you discontinue your current treatment. I only want to make you aware of the fact that the choices you make in your daily life have a direct impact on your health. Do you act in a manner that will produce good health and happiness? God's will is that you live a happy, healthy life. God's will is perfect. You still have that perfect will inside of you. Acknowledge and believe in your perfect will.

## SOUL PRINCIPLE

*It is God's will, or intention, that we live content, healthy, peaceful lives.*

—Dr. M. T. Morter, Jr.

### BOOSTER THOUGHT #2
### How do my thoughts affect my health?

Understand that thoughts are things, and furthermore that thoughts create things. What you meditate on, you actually create. Sounds simple today, but proving this concept on a scientific level has been somewhat difficult and only recently achieved. Quantum physics now shows that thoughts can literally alter the behavior of an electron. As a crude analogy, our aura is an electron cloud which contains spirit information. Webster defines aura as: 1) a distinctive atmosphere surrounding a given source; 2) a luminous radiation. I use the term "field" to describe the atmosphere in and around your body. Your field is made up of a combination of your soul and your spirit. Your field/spirit/soul is actually much more than your aura, but the aura is a physical manifestation of the field/spirit/soul. Kirlian photography captures the aura on film; some people can actually see auras. It is important here to acknowledge that the electrons of the aura are in your field and that the electron behavior of your aura can be altered by your mind. Again, thanks to Dr. Valerie Hunt for her work in this area.

It is also necessary to understand that your field actually controls your body. Once you acknowledge and believe this, then it's easy to see that what you think about, you bring about. What you believe, you achieve. If you think about getting cancer, pray not to get cancer, or become consumed with not getting the cancer your mother has, then you are actually bringing cancer into your field. You actually arrange the electrons in your field in a way that creates cancer or whatever condition you meditate upon, even if you don't want it. You anatomically and atomically bring about what you think about by arranging the information to create either health or disease. It's your choice how you think.

Think and pray in a positive mode. Be thankful for your perfect health. Be grateful for your healthy, pink lungs, or your vibrant, rejuvenating blood supply. Thank God for your ability to walk, talk, reason, smell, hear, or feel. Offer positive appreciation for your healthy state of being. This will serve to maintain or bring about good health.

## SOUL PRINCIPLE

*Your thoughts create your soul energy field and affect*
*everything about your very existence.*

—Dr. M. T. Morter, Jr.

**BOOSTER THOUGHT #3**
**Do my thoughts affect God?**

No, there is nothing you can do to affect God. You can't change him and you can't barter with him or do anything that will alter him at all. No amount of money or reverence will change God or his way. As I have said many times, he is perfect, intense, and omnipotent.

Everything was created by God. God's master program runs the universe. All that he has created is perfect. Man has the ability to desecrate his human temple, his body, to such an extent that he lowers the vitality of his body, which allows germs to penetrate and permeate his physical body. When this happens, we often call the germs "bad germs." In reality, they are not bad at all; they are perfect. It's just that maybe they should be in the garden making carrots instead of in your lungs making tuberculosis or pneumonia. It is not the fault of the germ that your resistance is so low that it can grow there. In fact, tuberculosis or pneumonia is a perfect response to the condition you have created in your body. In this case, what you need to do is determine what you did to allow this condition to occur, not what you need to do to kill the bad germ.

Nothing you do affects God. Everything you do affects God's performance within you. Your choices in the Six Essentials for Life—what you eat and drink, how you exercise and rest, what you breathe and think—determine your level of health. These are conscious choices on your part and the responses to these choices are automatic. God/the spirit/nature reacts instantly to every choice you make. This natural force of energy responds for your survival. You act, nature responds. All in the name of survival.

There is only one response to any given action. That response will always be the same for that specific situation. You are not in control of these responses, nor do you affect God/nature/the spirit. Yet, the effect God's power can have on *you* is profound. All you have to do is acknowledge the power, believe in the power, and *know*, without a shadow of doubt, that this power is within you all the time. Then your life will change in such a way that you will live in a higher level of awareness. You will not feel the need to defend your way of life. You will be enveloped in a sense of peace that epitomizes a grander enlightenment. You will find within you a safe place or sanctuary that you can go to in order to reconnect with the spirit and you will know and trust the ultimate energy source to such a degree that you will no longer question or doubt any part of this wisdom. When you reach this level of consciousness, you will have arrived at a place of freedom. Your thoughts will be those of thankfulness and your response to life will be "It's okay." You will lose the desire to judge others. Your spiritual development will have transcended the physical realm and reached the summit of godliness.

While this may sound lofty and surreal, it is actually very real. It is a state of being that surpasses this physical world, a state of existence that knows that this drama we call our life lasts for only a second in the great play of eternity. This higher level of consciousness is available to each and every one of you. For centuries now, great philosophers, authors, and teachers have espoused on this subject. Today there are many books available to aid you in this quest. Among the finest I have read is Wayne Dyer's *Manifest Your Destiny*.[23]

## SOUL PRINCIPLE

*God's spirit is perfect and constant, thus not affected by anything else.*

—Dr. M. T. Morter, Jr.

**BOOSTER THOUGHT #4**
**Develop an attitude of "It's okay."**

I teach the "It's okay" concept at my professional seminars and health retreats. Keep in mind that your attitude has a huge impact on your life. If you think negatively, then you bring on negativity, while thinking positively creates positivity in your life. It's all in the attitude. Basically, there are three phases to the "It's okay" concept.

First is the past. In general, I have found that people tend to worry about the past. Many people try to forget unpleasant past experiences, which is not possible. So instead, they recall them and worry that things didn't go as they should have. "I should have done this. Or, I should not have done that. If I had only said this. Or, what if I had not said that?" It's a case of should've, would've, could've. You get the picture. The fact is, the past is just that—past. It's behind you. You can't change it because it's over. The only thing you can do about the past is to learn from it. Recall the event you tend to worry about and apply the three steps of forgiveness to it. See the good in it. Learn the lesson, and move on. Understand that "It's okay." Your past is okay.

The second phase to this concept is the present. I find that most people are anxious over their present state. They are in some form of anxiety, stress, or tension over their current existence. Again, know that your present state is okay. Focus on what you are all about and see the plan that God has for you and all of creation. Stay on the spiritual path; live on purpose, fulfilling your purpose in life. Be positive. It's okay.

Third is the future. Most people seem to fear the future; they are afraid of what the future may hold. "What if this happens or that happens? What if I get this disease or that disease? What if I lose my job or my money?" Many people live in fear of the "what ifs." If you are in this category, know that the future is okay. You can overcome the fear of the future by focusing on what you want, not what you don't want. Remember, you bring about what you think about. Think about the positive things you want for yourself and your family in the future. Emit positive thoughts about what your future holds. You will actually put them into existence. Again, it's okay.

## SOUL PRINCIPLE

*Relax and know that everything that has happened already is in the past and cannot be changed. You can change the future by your actions today. It's okay.*

—Dr. M. T. Morter, Jr.

# Thoughts on Relationships

### BOOSTER THOUGHT #1
### You attract your relationships

Your relationships are a direct reflection of your inner thoughts, attitudes, and feelings. Let me explain what I mean by that. As has already been established, you are an energy being. You radiate and pulsate with energy. Your energy field extends into infinity; however, the closer to your body, the more individualized it becomes. It is a combination of your soul and spirit, your aura, your electron cloud, and your electromagnetic energy field. This electron cloud surrounding you contains all the information to run your body. As has also been established, your energy field attracts to it similar energy from the universe. We are *all* made up of energy—we *all* attract like-energy to us.

This means that, among other things, you actually attract people to you who are like you as a result of the energy that you put out into the world. That's right—you attract your relationships. The people you attract have the same type of energy that you do. All you need to do to determine what type of energy you emit is to take a glance at your relationships. In other words, are you surrounded by positive-thinking, happy, healthy individuals? If so, then you are most likely attracting them to you as a result of the positive energy that you put out. On the other hand, if most of your relationships are with unhappy, negative, and grouchy people, then you are probably surrounded by these people because you are radiating with negative energy and actions that attract them to you. Happy attracts happy. Gloomy attracts gloomy.

But, you say, "I have some of the most negative people in my life, and I am not a negative person." Really? Think about it. Be honest with yourself. Listen to what you say and what you think.

Truly evaluate your inner thoughts and feelings. You may need to admit that your thinking needs some adjusting toward the positive side of the scale. This is not to say that I am placing blame or asking you to feel guilty. Not at all. I am merely asking you to be honest with yourself in order to identify the energy that you radiate into the world around you.

Your family, or those you have close relationships with or live with, are directly affected by your energy field, just as you are affected by their energy fields. A baby who is sick and cranky is being affected by the mother's field, as the mother is being affected by the baby's field. The negative, bossy father is also affecting his family. Sometimes a baby's energy field is disturbed at birth, due to forceps or other damaging influences at delivery. This can result in an ill baby or one who cries almost constantly. The soul energy is just no longer connected with the spirit energy. A separation has taken place and must be addressed in order to regain the harmony of soul and spirit.

I have worked with many colicky or cranky babies to balance their body's energy fields. At the same time I typically find it necessary to work with the mother to help her regain balance and symmetry in her own body. The relationship between the mother and infant is vital to the health and vitality of the infant, since the mother's energy field has the biggest influence on the infant's energy field. However, it is often the father who upsets the mother, who in turn upsets the infant. And so the cycle goes. Harmony—it's all about harmony.

Your energy field is directly in control of your health and your relationships. As we live our daily lives we influence our field by the way we respond to the stresses of life. If we respond with anger, hate, or frustration we will create an energy in our field that will attract relationships that will make us angry, hateful or frustrated. When you feel these emotions, recall this old adage—he who gets upset is the one who has the problem. Realize that your relationships may represent a part of you that needs to be changed.

As adults, our family is often based on the way we were raised as children. Feelings from our past experiences manifest in our present life. We tend to act and react the same way our parents did. You may be thinking that you don't like the way your parents acted and that you don't want to be the way they were or are. How can you change your life so that you do not respond in the manner that your parents did?

First, change the feelings you put into your field. One issue of major importance here is judgment. You must overcome the urge to place judgment on your parents, boss, husband, wife, children, or other significant individuals in your life. I am not saying you can forget the way these people treated you in the past or how they may treat you today. I am saying that you must not judge them for their actions. You can't change the past or the way anyone else acts. You are only responsible for your *own* actions and reactions.

What *can* you do? Observe the actions of others. Don't judge, but rather observe and learn. Make a decision on how you will live your life according to the observations you have made. Instead of judging and thinking, "My dad did it all wrong as a father," think this: "As a result of growing up with my father, I am going to be a more loving, caring, thoughtful father." You can turn it around to your benefit. Let your experiences be your teachers and benefit from the lessons each experience offers. Live your life today in a way that will insure that your future is as happy and harmonious as you want it to be.

## SOUL PRINCIPLE

*In order to attract positive, caring relationships, I must be a positive, caring person.*

—Dr. M. T. Morter, Jr.

### BOOSTER THOUGHT #2
### Happy Mother's Day

Earlier I shared with you the story of my daughter-in-law and her feelings about having enough love for many babies. Recall that she felt extreme love toward baby Sarah during the pregnancy and thereafter. Sarah was developed in a loving, caring field inside of her mother, then treated with love after she was born. Remember the letter that was written to baby Sarah? Well, I'd like to share a letter that Sarah, now sixteen years old, just wrote to her mother.

> *Dear Mom,*
>
> *Hey, well I didn't know what to do for you for Mother's Day, so I decided to write you a letter to tell you how much I appreciate you. You are always here for me. You listen to what I have to say, and you understand what I mean. I know that if I ever needed anything that you would help me. I go to you with all of my problems. You are one of my best friends.*
>
> *I know some of the things that I do have let you down, and I want you to know that I am trying. I don't like letting you down. You did a great job teaching me wrong from right. Don't worry about me, I am*

*doing fine. You have put a good head on my shoulders, and you and dad have set a great example. Thank you so much for everything that you have done and do.*

*I love you,*
*Sarah*

It seems obvious to me that the relationship between this mother and daughter is a good one, one that has been bonded in love since the beginning of development. Relationships grow and change over time. Your energy field develops and changes, too. You have control over what you put into your field with your thoughts, actions, and reactions. So you have control over what type of relationships you attract. If you want to have a better relationship with your daughter, son, mother, father, or anyone else, you may need to change some things about yourself first. Your relationships are an extension of and expression of *you*. If you don't like what you see in your relationships, you may be seeing a part of yourself that you would like to change. You are only responsible for your own actions, thoughts, and feelings. When you are positive, loving, and caring, your relationships will be, too.

## SOUL PRINCIPLE

*Your relationships are an extension of and expression of*
*YOU.*

—Dr. M. T. Morter, Jr.

# Thoughts on Loneliness

### BOOSTER THOUGHT #1
### He was always there

When she looks back on it today, it's hard believe that her life had gotten so out of control. It seemed that everything she did caused something bad to happen. Everywhere she turned things were getting messed up; nothing ever seemed to go right. Murphy's Law was ruling her life, or so it seemed at the time. She was just so lonely. Having friends was what she thought she needed. Being accepted by a new group of friends would make her feel better.

Jill had grown up in a small Midwestern community. Her mother and father were decent people. They loved her, but they were not demonstrative in doing so. They rarely hugged or showed their affection. She had most everything she needed as a child, except for an occasional hug or pat on the back. This is not to say that Jill was mistreated or abused. She just didn't grow up feeling truly loved. There seemed to be something missing in her life. She was lonely—not alone, but lonely.

After high school graduation, she moved to a neighboring state to attend college. Her parents helped her and her friend from high school move their things into their new room. They even offered to walk with them to orientation class. Jill refused their offer, thanked them, and they were off. Now, she felt, her life could begin. She was scared, but ready.

Classes started about a week later and everything seemed to be going well. In fact, Jill made some new friends during the first week. She quickly became quite popular. She had invitations to dinner, dancing, and parties almost every night. This was a new experience for her and one that she was enjoying. It felt good to have all these friends. She really wanted everyone to like her. Her roommate, Gina, didn't seem to be quite so popular. Jill brought her along a few times, but her old friend didn't seem to like her new friends. Gina soon began to decline the invitations, choosing to do her own thing. Out from under the constraints of her parents, Jill chose to accept most of the invitations. She told herself it was fun and really quite harmless. And it was fun, for awhile.

Since she was only a freshman; she was introduced to a lot of new things—things like alcohol and drugs. The first few sips of beer were terrible, but she stuck with it until she actually acquired a taste for it. It became a regular habit, in fact. She would go to class and then meet her new buddies at the bar that was noted for never checking identification. There they would sit until they had "caught a buzz" and then they'd take off for the next party. She was even too busy partying to remember to eat. She would sometimes go days without eating anything. It even got to the point that eating made her sick. It didn't really seem like a problem, quite the opposite really. She was losing weight and thought she looked better than ever.

It was not long after this routine was developed that Jill was turned on to drugs. At first it was marijuana, then it moved on to cocaine and other drugs. Night after night they partied. Day after day she went without eating. It seemed okay, as long as she was attending class and keeping her grades up. And so it went on like this for a few months. She told herself it was no big deal, everyone was doing it. Everybody she knew got high and drank beer until the wee hours of the morning. Everybody was really skinny. And that was true—for the people that she knew. It's just that she didn't know everybody. There were a lot people at that college who didn't behave that way.

Her roommate was one of those people. She would try to talk to Jill, but Jill didn't want to listen to her. She thought she was just jealous of her new-found popularity. And so Jill continued with her wild forays. When she went home for Thanksgiving her parents noticed that she had lost weight and her dad noted that she "had lost her baby fat." They all laughed and Jill was convinced that she looked great.

When she got back to school the parties started back up. She partied so late that she couldn't make it to class. In fact, she went one whole week without attending any classes at all. On those mornings she would wake up and get high before getting out of bed. Her first drink of the day was a Bloody Mary. On it went like this until something happened that made her world come tumbling down.

She woke up and saw the policeman reaching for her arm. He was kneeling by her side. She could only vaguely see him. It was like something was over her eyes. She brought her hand to her eyes to wipe it away and saw that it was blood. Her head was pounding. She tried to sit up, but he told her to lie still. Her whole body was aching and she was confused. It took a few minutes for the memories of what had happened to her to come rushing back. She had been raped.

She remembered meeting the guy in the bar. He was so nice to her while they were there. It wasn't until they got outside that he began to turn sour. He got mad at her for walking too slowly and he had started to yell at her. Then, he hit her in the head with something and grabbed her by the arm. She remembered him dragging her into the alley; she remembered the rape. She even remembered crying for him not to leave her like that. The last thing she saw was his fist flying toward her face.

The next few weeks were a blur. The hospital, the police reports, her parents coming to take her home. Then another hospital and more tests being run. The intravenous feedings, the minister, the doctors and nurses, her parents crying. And the loneliness. Oh, the loneliness.

She arrived home on a Saturday morning in late December. The weather was crisp and it was beginning to snow. Her dad built a fire and her mother wrapped an afghan around her shoulders as she sat and stared at the dancing flames. They were both so concerned for her. They had hardly left her side during the whole ordeal. Her mother had not attended any of her regular meetings or kept any appointments. Her dad had taken as many days off from work as was possible. They loved her. They really loved her, and she realized that they had *always* loved her. It was then that it came to her, as if in a flash. She could sit, mope, and feel sorry for herself or she could pull herself up and start over.

She recognized that this was the first day in the rest of her life. This was a day that could be filled with positive, loving thoughts that would help to heal her wounded soul. She stood and reached out to her mother with open arms and her mother came to her. Their embrace brought tears to both of their eyes. When her dad walked into the room, he hesitantly approached, then encircled them both with his loving arms. The threesome stood locked in that embrace for several minutes. They all felt the power of the fourth entity in their circle—God. No one said anything. They didn't have to. She realized during that time that not only had they not hugged her, but she had never hugged them. They never knew that she really needed their hugs. Now, with unspoken terms, they understood. The spiritual energy flowed among them, mending and healing each of their souls.

That was the day that Jill turned her life around. That was the day that she came to know that she was never alone. That not only her parent's love, but also God's spirit and love were always with her. She knew then that she would never feel lonely again. She knew she didn't need anyone else to make her soul peaceful, that what she needed dwelt within her. It is from the times of deepest darkness that comes the most profound enlightenment— whether in the form of a sudden epiphany or a gradual awareness. She knew right then that in times of need she could remember and relive the power of that fateful embrace.

## SOUL PRINCIPLE

*God's spirit is always with you.*

—Dr. M. T. Morter, Jr.

**BOOSTER THOUGHT #2**
**A family's grief**

The following story relates the feelings shared by the family of one of my former patients.

It was upon taking our seven-year-old daughter, Leslie, to the doctor for a broken arm that it was discovered that she had cancer. As a father, this was very frightening. Almost immediately we began chemotherapy; we saw prominent experts in the field. The chemotherapy was extremely hard on her. She was much too sensitive to the affects of the treatment. While sixteen treatments were recommended, the doctors decided that she would be unable to make it past the sixth or seventh session due to her extreme sensitivity. The doctors gave her little to no hope. That is when we began our trek to other countries—Mexico and Germany—willing to do anything to save our little girl.

We first saw Dr. Morter on a television infomercial. We brought our daughter to see him, but the changes and improvements we saw were too late in coming. Dr. Morter worked with her to remove interference between her soul and her spirit, allowing to be what would be. We wanted to protect her, to get a miracle. We all prayed for a miracle. Dr. Morter told us all along that the power was God's power and that he could not heal her, only help to remove any interference that was present. All our prayers for a miracle didn't produce one. On the conscious level, we all wanted her to live. On the subconscious level, she was in tune with God. Perhaps it is that she had already decided to go and meet her maker. For whatever reason, she passed away.

When we lost our darling daughter, each of us had an enormous feeling of failure. The depression was almost overwhelming. I would think of the things we used to do together. She had become only a memory. Being quite spiritual and religious, I was devastated by her death. She was a special child, very intelligent, seemingly older than her age. We found out about her cancer when she was only seven. After she died, we wondered how God could do this to us. If he was going to take her away so soon, why did he give her to us in the first place? Now we know why.

After her death, it was a very difficult time. I still believed in the Lord, but I felt stabbed in the back, let down. Our whole family felt the same way. The grief produced such an empty feeling— we were all quite miserable, twenty-four hours per day. The predominate feeling was one of failure. Failure as a father, a mother, a sister, and a brother. We felt as if she would have stayed had we been better at our roles. My wife would say that if she had been a better mother, had loved her even more, perhaps Leslie would have stayed with us. I felt the same way. Our teenaged children felt that they should have been better siblings. We blamed ourselves somehow. We were afraid to do anything, for fear of messing things up. This caused our self-confidence to plummet. Overcoming these feelings was not easy, but it was necessary for each of us, in order to maintain a high quality of life. We couldn't go through the rest of our lives feeling depressed and guilty.

Immediately following the funeral, my wife reported to me that she had no good memories of Leslie, only bad ones. Nothing beyond the sickness and the pain. She said her soul energy was blackened by the death. She, like each of us, had to work to get her soul back in tune with her spirit, to lighten the soul. Our understanding of Dr. Morter's philosophy helped us to change. I turned to God; I screamed at him. I wanted to know how he could have done this to us. But I came to know that he still loved me. We began to have some good memories. One good memory led to another one and faith led to more good memories. God was in control.

We now have many wonderful memories and know that Leslie touched a lot of hearts and lives. Now we know that her life was a beautiful one. The last time she was hospitalized, mainly for the pain, I told her that if she saw Jesus to go to him; she did just that. It was meant to be. Even though she was ready to go and I had given her the encouragement, if it had not been her time then she would not have been accepted. She would have been sent back to us, to get better and live. However, it *was* her time. Her life on earth was over.

God is an important part of our lives, and life is getting better. We can talk to God again. We still go to her grave to feel closer to her, but we know that she is not really there. She is now everywhere, all the time. She is in this room with me right now. We have learned that it is most important that we remember her with loving memories. We feel much better having gotten our thoughts and emotions in perspective. We each felt such extreme grief, but we have been able to reduce that overwhelming feeling. This concept helps to get us through each day:

*I'm better today and I'll be even better tomorrow.*
*Every day is a better day.*

The time of grief is different for everyone. We were very close to Leslie; we focused so much of our attention on her for the last two years of her life. The fear of her death was a part of our daily life. We have to feel good about the decisions we made all along the way. We only wish we had known about Dr. Morter earlier; we might have had a different outcome. However, we did the best we could. It is the way it is supposed to be.

Several good things have happened that directly relate to Leslie's life. A couple at the funeral had a very sick baby. Watching them care for the baby and listening to the baby cry, made us realize that we could pass on some of the things we had learned in caring for a sick child. One of the things we recommended was that they take their baby to see a doctor trained by Dr. Morter. They did this and the baby improved, almost immediately. The interference was removed and the baby is now much better. It felt so good and was very enlightening to have helped them.

Another wonderful occurrence came about with the doctor who first diagnosed Leslie with cancer. This man was the last one to leave the funeral. He told us that he and his wife were undecided about having children until they met our daughter. Now, he said, they truly understand the meaning of family. One would think that watching us experience the grief of death would lead them away from wanting children. However, he expressed that the true importance and impact of unconditional love that they witnessed in our family during this difficult time actually led them to decide to have children of their own. This is such a touching occurrence for us. We are eternally warmed that we could have such an affect on others.

Looking back, it's easier to note the pearls of wisdom revealed to us. One such bit of knowledge is that we should enjoy life and loved ones each and every day. Be thankful for the time you have with those you love, for you don't know when that time may end. Our teenaged son says that in the last months of her life he learned not to "make fun of her." It was extremely touching to see him holding her and kissing her. In the last days of her life, it was also interesting to note that Leslie often wanted to do something nice for someone else. After a visit from a special aunt, she would say, "Mom, we should get something nice for her." And we noticed that both of our teenaged children began to think of others before themselves. It was a time of grief, a time of growth, and a time that none of us will ever forget.

So, enjoy your loved ones. Be kind to them. Do the things with them that you would like to do *today*. Take the time to show them and tell them that you care. Love them more.

The most important advice that we could give to others who are grieving the death of a loved one is to think of the good memories. You get to choose what you remember, so remember the good times, the loving embraces, the small acts of kindness, and the special glances. When you feel overcome with the loss, or find yourself questioning the fairness of it all, remember that you are better off for having had that person in your life. Even though you may have liked for it to have lasted longer, be thankful for the time you had. Know that even if you feel very lonely during this time, you are not alone. You may be separated from

God and his energy source at this time. Turning to the good memories, the positive memories, will bring you back in touch with him. Know that God is with you all the time.

Leslie's birth, her existence, the loving memories, the amazing affect she had on others, the strength of character we gained through her life and her death, and the knowledge and insight that we now share within our family all serve as gentle reminders of the awesome power of God's unconditional love.

## SOUL PRINCIPLE

*Make each day count, expressing your unconditional love for others.*

—Dr. M. T. Morter, Jr.

**BOOSTER THOUGHT #3**
**Divine homesickness**

While I have stated throughout this book that physical ailments and diseases begin in the mind, I feel it is imperative that I reiterate those concepts here. We first notice a symptom or condition in the physical plane but, typically, the cause of that complaint lies in the mental realm. Negative thinking that is bonded with strong emotions like hatred, anger, jealousy, fear, and loneliness produces a black or negative energy. It actually causes an interference in the free-flow of the soul's energy within you. In addition, your body produces chemicals in response to the emotion. The combination of the chemicals and the blockage of energy creates sickness, malaise, and disease.

Loneliness accompanies many, if not most, diseases and illnesses. When we get sick or hurt, we feel afraid and alone—like we are the only one with this particular ailment. It seems that this is the most severe thing that has ever happened to us. It is specific and personal to our individual, lone being. We sometimes revel in our unique condition or symptom. But it is the feeling of uniqueness or individuality paired with the negativity that creates the feeling of loneliness, detachment, separateness, or isolation. Many people have shared with me that their disease or condition left them feeling all alone, even in a room crowded with people.

I believe that this feeling of loneliness is actually a manifestation of the separation of the soul from the spirit—divine homesickness. It is the way we express the separation from our creative energy force. Negative emotions, chemical responses, and blocked energy flow guarantee this separation. As long as you are in this state of being—negative, with interference in the flow of your energy—you will not be able to reach true harmony between your soul and the divine spiritual energy that created you and is still in your body ready to heal you.

This is not to say that someone who is dying of a disease cannot reach this spiritual harmony. By turning to God, the spiritual energy source, and recognizing him as the divine power, anyone can reach this exalted state. It is the belief, actually the knowing, that God is the ultimate force that will relieve feelings of negativity, such as loneliness. We need to acknowledge that there is a master plan and that we are only a small part of it. We don't have to know all that God knows, we just have to know that God knows. We can either flow in unison with the plan or we can fight against it by trying to create our own plan. It is the resistance to the grand plan, the pulling away from the divine energy source, that produces malaise, sickness, and disease. When you understand that there is a source of power many times greater than you and that this powerful source has a design and a plan for all things, great and small, then you will be enveloped in a state of peace. You will begin to function, think, and act in a way that not only acknowledges, but amplifies, that power. As you accept and know this spiritual realm you will attract peace, harmony, and love. The benefit you gain will be reciprocal; as you give, so shall you receive.

## SOUL PRINCIPLE

*Loneliness is an expression of separation between soul and spirit.*

—Dr. M. T. Morter, Jr.

# Dr. Morter's Belief Builders
## PRESCRIPTIONS FOR THE MENTAL PLANE

- If it is to be, it is up to me.
- Nothing is good or bad, but thinking makes it so.
- I cannot learn what I think I already know.
- It is not what is said that hurts me, but how I respond to what is said.
- I am a chained slave to anyone I hate.
- The only thing I can truly ever change is my mind.
- My positive thoughts attract positivity in my life.
- What I think determines who I am.
- Thoughts are things.
- Thoughts are energy.
- Thoughts create things.
- Negative thoughts affect me in a negative way.
- My health and happiness are dependent on me.
- My mind matters.
- I must see the good and learn the lessons from each experience in my life.
- I am totally responsible for how I feel.
- Love more, expect less.
- I cannot use my mind to deceive my perfect innate intelligence; it is not possible to do so.
- My thinking can interfere with my spiritual path.
- I may be lonely, but I am never alone; the creative energy is always with me.
- Forgiveness means to give up the chance to get even.
- I learn something from everyone I meet and every experience of my life.
- Everything in my life has a lesson to teach.
- I must see the good in each event in my life.
- Things don't happen *to* me, they happen *for* me— to learn a lesson.
- Positive mental imaging will bring positive elements into being.

- If I can conceive it, I can achieve it.
- Judgment is merely the rating of someone or something according to one's own beliefs.
- I will love others for what they are, not what I want them to be.
- Judgment occurs when I want others to see things my way.
- I will judge not, lest I be judged.
- Learn the lesson of the moment.
- My mind is my attractor; what I think about I am.
- Every disease is an expression of a suppressed emotion.
- Judgment creates my soul.
- What I see in the world, I become.
- If I don't sow it, I will never reap it.
- I will attract that which I radiate.
- Putting enough love in my heart will allow the part of me that is diseased to be healed.
- The steps of forgiveness can and will change my life forever.
- I don't have to be right—or wrong.

# CHAPTER 5

# THE SPIRITUAL PLANE

> Great men are they who see that spiritual
> is stronger than any material force—that
> thoughts rule the world.
> —Ralph Waldo Emerson

It is the spiritual plane that holds the answers to the universe. This plane created the master program or grand design. This is the plane which contains innate intelligence, chi, *prana*, the life force. The spiritual plane is omnipotent, omnipresent, and everlasting. It created the heavens and the universe and all living beings and inanimate objects. The spiritual plane is responsible for the relationships between all of these creations. The spiritual plane is God, Buddha, Allah, the King, or whatever else you prefer to call it. It is the almighty power and energy; it is unchanging, perpetual, and eternal.

This spirit created you and lives within you. As I said in Chapter 2, I believe the "empty space" inside your body is actually made up of spiritual information, which is responsible for communication between your individual cells, you totally, and the almighty spirit.

It is the goal of this section of Booster Thoughts to help you learn to integrate your soul and your spirit in order to attain a higher level of health—to become at peace, as one, with your creator. I will teach you that you can walk in harmony with the spiritual path. Lessons on faith, prayer, recognizing and utilizing the universal consciousness, and believing in your perfect self are given in an attempt to help you reach your optimum level of health, happiness, and success—using sound, scientific, quantum principles.

I want you to learn to *give in* to the power that is in you. Learn to get your conscious mind out of the way, to make way for spiritual awareness. Create peace with your mind so you can open your heart and your eyes to a different way of thinking. When you become aware and begin to believe, then you know, without a shadow of doubt, that you are on that spiritual path leading to your ultimate state of health, happiness, and success.

# Thoughts on Faith

### BOOSTER THOUGHT #1
### The bike ride

This story cleverly depicts the role of God in the life of the author.

At first I saw God as an observer, like my judge, keeping track of things I did wrong. This way, God would know whether I merited heaven or hell when I died. He was always out there, sort of like the President. I recognized His picture when I saw it, but I didn't really know Him at all.

But later on, when I recognized my higher power better, it seemed as though life was rather like a bike ride, on a tandem bike, and I noticed God was in the back helping me pedal.

I don't know when it was that He suggested we change places, but life has not been the same since... life with my higher power, that is, making life much more exciting.

When I had control, I knew the way. It was rather boring but predictable. It was always the shortest distance between the points.

But when He took the lead, He knew delightful cuts, up mountains, and through rocky places and at breakneck speeds; it was all I could do to hang on! Even though it looked like madness, He kept saying, "Pedal, pedal!"

I worried and became anxious, asking, "Where are you taking me?" He just laughed and didn't answer, and I found myself starting to trust. I soon forgot my boring life and entered into the adventure, and when I'd say, "I'm scared," He'd lean back and touch my hand.

He took me to people with gifts that I needed; gifts of healing, acceptance and joy. They gave me their gifts to take on my journey. *Our* journey, that is, God's and mine.

And we were off again. He said, "Give the gifts away, they're extra baggage, too much weight." So I did, to the people we met, and I found that in giving I received, and still our burden was light.

I did not trust Him at first, in control of my life. I thought He'd wreck it. But He knew *bike secrets*, knew how to make it bend to take sharp corners, jump to clear places filled with rocks, fly to shorten scary passages.

And I'm learning to shut up and pedal in the strangest places, and I'm beginning to enjoy the view and the cool breeze on my face with my delightful constant companion, *my higher power.*

And when I'm sure I can't go on anymore, He just smiles and says, "Pedal …"

—*Author Unknown*

## SOUL PRINCIPLE

*Have faith that God is with you all the time.*

—Dr. M. T. Morter, Jr.

### BOOSTER THOUGHT #2
### What does God have to do with my health?

This is a very good question. Many people pray to God to cure their condition whenever they get sick, but it doesn't seem to work. Then they assume there is no God, that God is not listening to them, or that they are deserving of this condition and God is punishing them for the sins they have committed. That is the logic that many people go through. Some people even turn away from God and say, "I knew there was no God. I prayed for his help and he didn't give it."

On the contrary, I believe that every prayer is answered and that every thought is a silent prayer. Think about what you think about. Pray in a fashion that will actually bring what you want into your energy field. Instead of being judgmental, be thankful. Have faith that God is a loving God and know that he is a universal power and intelligence that flows through you, as well as everything else. He is the inspiration, the creator, and he is non-judgmental.

When you think about God in this manner, you will come to realize that, while you are not God, he is in you and you are an expression of his creation. You are actually in charge of yourself and your health is an expression of your conscious choices. You are an element of and a creation of the omnipotent force we call God; you are a carrier of this eternal force. Think of God as the ultimate playwright and yourself as the one playing the part of his spirit. Having faith in God means having faith in yourself. While you are *not* God, he is *in* you.

My desire is to turn you on to your own powers. I want you to understand that it is not necessary to separate yourself from God by creating a soul that is different from the spirit, as mankind so often does. Getting beyond this idea of separation and evolving to a higher level of consciousness is what this book is all about. Look within yourself to find that you have everything within you that you need to reach this ultimate level of awareness. Love and accept this unseen power that you hold. If you act with your heart and your nature, instead of your mind, then you will begin to develop an inner knowledge that will accelerate the process of your development. Moving to this higher level of awareness is more of a shedding process than an adding process.

Keep in mind that the order of nature is not always a pattern that you might expect. The form of mountains, streams, clouds, trees, and even people is varied and sometimes crooked; but it is always perfect. We, as humans, often want to change things to fit an organized symmetrical mold. This is not the way of nature. Nature allows for variations, for an unfolding or flowing that is a perfect part of the grand plan. We need to relax and accept this natural process.

# SOUL PRINCIPLE

*Trusting in the spiritual, godly powers of the universe is experiencing faith or "knowingness."*

—Dr. M. T. Morter, Jr.

## BOOSTER THOUGHT #3
### Learning the lesson and seeing the good

To me the mission of life is very simple: to learn the lesson of the moment. If you do this, judgment is not necessary. Jealousy, hate, anger, fear, guilt, shame, despair, depression, cancer, arthritis, jaundice, colitis, the flu, and all other maladies become unnecessary when you truly learn life's lesson. When you open your eyes to the spiritual plane, you reach a place where your maladies are no longer needed for your survival. In fact, it is no longer even possible to display these discomforts or diseases. The concept of learning the lessons life offers is not unique. In fact, many have avowed this to be one of the most valuable precepts of life.

It is interesting to note here that for several hundred years after the death of Jesus, the Christian religion believed in reincarnation. Reincarnation is defined as the belief that the soul survives after death and is reborn in the body of another person or some other living thing. It was finally banished from the Christian faith, for the obvious reason of control on the part of the leaders at that time. It was felt that if people had the freedom to think that they were coming back to earth again, then they could do whatever they wanted during this lifetime. They would just come back and get it right the next time.

Reincarnation is also called transmigration of the soul. It was a fundamental belief of the ancient Greeks and is still a part of Buddhism, Hinduism, Jainism, Sikhism, and other religions that originated in India. It is also the doctrine of some of the modern spiritualist movements. This is not to say that these religions or movements deem it satisfactory to misbehave during this life. But it is believed by some theologians today that the leaders of the Christian faith removed reincarnation from the religion for that reason.

Here are my concepts regarding reincarnation. We are all built with God's wisdom, using physical material that existed before our existence. Understand that the smallest physical material, even smaller than electrons, was here before we were and all of this material contains information of God's creation. Since all matter has been here since the beginning, in some form or other, the material we are made of has been involved with many experiences. How can you explain a two-year-old child capable of playing a piano with concert ability—unless he inherited this ability from previous experiences recorded in universal consciousness. This may not be *the* answer, but it is one. I do know for sure that we are all made of electrons that existed before and may have been altered by previous minds, creating different souls. Maybe, just maybe, this youngster received enough of these special electrons that contained the capability to play a piano or maybe that person came here to experience this ability. For certain, there is an answer to this phenomenon. It may just be beyond our conscious ability to fully understand it. Keep in mind that we are all unique individuals with unique abilities, sharing a common ancestor called God. When we walk on his path we can express these abilities to the maximum.

Many organized religions want to control their followers. They do not like for their people to have freedom, but rather to adhere to strict theosophies and to closely follow the advice of the leaders of the religion. Ironically enough, in a time when more people are experiencing spiritual epiphanies, the attendance at mainline churches is down. These churches also report a decrease in financial support. Could it be that the church does not offer what the people need? A Gallup poll recently showed that thirty-three percent of the population studied reported a personal spiritual experience. According to some, this number could be even higher, since many people do not feel at ease in reporting such personal experiences. So approximately one-third of the population of the United States has had a "personal spiritual experience," yet the attendance and support of the mainline church is decreasing. This is an interesting state of affairs. There must be a reason.

My experience has revealed that the greater a person is involved with his religion, the less tolerant he is of other religions, and also the more judgmental he is. As I have said, judgment is harmful to your health. It doesn't matter whether you are judging others for their sexual preferences, the color of their skin, their religion, or their politics. Judgment is judgment. It can, and most likely will, result in disease, discomfort, or some form of ailment, whether mental or physical.

If you truly learn the lessons life brings to you, as they occur, then you will be able to see the good in each experience. Even if the situation causes you pain or discomfort, you must see how this is actually good for you, and thus learn the lesson that it has appeared to teach you. For instance, if Uncle Joe has abused you for years, learn the lesson that this experience is trying to teach you. What might that be? Maybe you experienced this abuse as a demonstration of how *not* to treat others. Maybe you lived through it so that you could help others who suffered the same. When you understand the lesson, learn from the lesson, and see the good in it, you will know exactly what the right answers are for you and your situation. It could be as simple as, "Wow, I'm a better person for having experienced that." When you get it, you will know it and you will be better for it.

## SOUL PRINCIPLE

*When you truly "see the good" in an unpleasant experience,*
*then you will have simultaneously learned the lesson.*
—Dr. M. T. Morter, Jr.

# Thoughts on Prayer

### BOOSTER THOUGHT #1
### Fifty percent of gross

Experiences with prayer seem to run the gamut from concentrated formal study to "don't believe in it." Generally speaking, most of us have had some type of training on how, when, and what to pray. Our training varies from religion to religion, from household to household, and from person to person. You may have memorized various prayers in school or Sunday school. You might have been taught to repeat particular prayers for certain shortcomings on your part. You could have learned that whatever or however you prayed was okay, that since it's your personal relationship with God, you can say anything you want to say. You could have been taught that you should pray every evening before you go to sleep. You could have decided, from experience, that it is not important to pray at all. Experiences with prayer seem to be vast and varied.

But have you ever really thought about what and how you pray? I mean, how to structure your own prayer in order to *successfully* talk to God (or whatever you may call the ultimate spirit or creator). Do you *expect* something from your prayers? Why do you pray at all? Or don't you?

When I think about prayer I am often reminded of the movie, *The End*. Burt Reynolds plays the part of a desperate man who swims out into the ocean in an attempt to commit suicide. After he gets out into the deep waters, he has a change of heart. Suddenly, he begins to bargain with God. He says something like, "God, help me. Make me a better swimmer. If you help me I'll be a better man. I'll be a better father. I'll follow the Ten Commandments. I'll give you fifty percent of my gross income." However, by the time he reaches shore the promise has dropped to ten percent of net. While this makes for a funny movie line, it is all too representative of how many people pray.

Often, people think that praying to God is about bargaining or asking for what you *don't* want. "I'll start going to church every Sunday if you'll get me that raise." Or, "Please cure my cancer if I stop smoking right now." Or, how about, "Don't let me get Hodgkin's like my mother." "Don't let my arthritis get worse." Do any of these sound familiar?

So, how *should* we pray? Pray in a manner as though you are giving thanks for that which you are asking, as if you have already received it. Jesus told us how to gain our desires. In Mark 11:24, it states, "Therefore I say unto you, What things soever ye desire, when ye pray, believe that ye receive them, and ye shall have them." Create it *energetically* in the spiritual field, so that it may come to being in the physical world. You will actually help to make it happen by thinking it into reality. If you cannot envision your goals, they can never come to fruition. On the other hand, that which you think about, you bring about. And so it is with prayer. It's your choice how you pray.

The more you pray to God to cure your disease or ailment, the worse it is going to get, because you are putting negativity into your field. God doesn't know negativity; he only hears "cancer" or "arthritis," thus creating more cancer or arthritis. In perfection, there is no negativity. The spiritual energy works to create the positive outcome necessary for your survival. Cancer and arthritis are created as the results of choices made over a period of years. Each is the perfect response by the spiritual intellect for survival. So praying *not* to have them is futile. Your perfect, positive spirit only hears the positive. It doesn't pick up on *not* having "cancer;" only on having "cancer" (or whatever ailment you suffer from, mentally or physically).

Blaming God for not answering such a prayer is not right either. The spiritual energy is a positive, perfect power. Your goal is to resonate with that power. Keep in mind that your current condition is the result of the choices you have made in the past. To change your future, you need to change your choices today. Regardless of how you pray, God is not going to do anything any differently than he is doing right now. Since God is perfect all the time and is everywhere all the time, he is doing everything all the time. God never went anywhere, because He was already there. So, he can't do any more, no matter how you pray. You may have strayed from him and his path, but he didn't turn his back on you. You may have turned your back on him. If you pray in a positive fashion, then your prayers will be more effective.

For example, let's say that you have a skin rash. Your most effective prayer might go something like this: "Dear God, thank you for my perfect skin. My soft, supple, smooth skin is wonderful. Thank you for creating such a glorious system of elimination in my body." Then, see your skin as perfect. Understand the purpose of your skin, that your skin is a method by which you can eliminate toxins from your body. If you did not eliminate these toxins (which show up as your rash) then you would harbor the toxins within, causing some other organic or systemic problem. Your skin rash is your perfect response for eliminating the toxins within you. Furthermore, it is a signal to you that something is not right. Be thankful, truly thankful, that your body is designed to survive, that your body is designed to eliminate wastes through your skin, that your body has alerted you to notice that something is amiss. Your rash is your warning signal, as other symptoms warn for other diseases.

The skin rash is merely an example. Put your own discomfort in the place of the skin rash. Understand and be thankful for the perfection of your own ailment. See the good in it, and pray with thanks for its creation, as it has allowed you to survive thus far. I do not believe that our God is a punishing God. If you do not abide by the spiritual laws of nature, then you actually punish yourself. The result is pain, illness, disease, or depression. And, keep in mind, these are perfect responses to the choices you have made. The misery and disease in the world are man's creation, not God's. I know that he loves us all and wants each of us to join him. I know that he wants every one of us to walk in his spiritual path.

## SOUL PRINCIPLE

*Pray in a manner of thankfulness for that which you are praying, as though you have already received it.*

—Dr. M. T. Morter, Jr.

**BOOSTER THOUGHT #2**
**How do I know if my prayers have been answered?**

Every prayer is answered. Think about this: every thought is a silent prayer and every thought accumulates. Once it reaches a certain accumulation, it is answered. I once heard a conversation that went something like this: Joe said to his friend, "How do I know that God answers my prayers? I've been praying for something, but I haven't gotten it." His friend said, "Yeah, he answered you. He said no to you. That was your answer."

I do not believe that God ever says no. I believe he is always perfect and that there is no negativity in the spiritual world. Man may say no to his perfect spiritual path by not following it, by creating his own path, but God is steady, unchanging, unswerving—like the laser. He is simply waiting for us to get back on his spiritual path, to join him in the spiritual journey. Just as he never punishes, he never says no. Negativity is found only in the physical and mental planes, not in the spiritual one. He awaits the time that our soul path joins his spiritual one. It is our choice to make this happen again. God never turned his back on his creation. Man turned his back on God's creation.

## SOUL PRINCIPLE

*Every thought is a silent prayer.*

—Dr. M. T. Morter, Jr.

# Thoughts on Integrating Your Soul with the Spirit

### BOOSTER THOUGHT #1
**Footprints**

One night a man had a dream. He dreamt he was walking along the beach with the Lord. Across the sky flashed scenes from his life. For each scene he noticed two sets of footprints on the sand—one belonging to him and the other to the Lord. When the last scene had flashed before him, he looked back at the footprints and he noticed that many times along the path there was only one set. He also noticed that this happened during the lowest and saddest times of his life. This bothered him and he questioned the Lord. "Lord, you said that once I decided to follow you, you would walk all the way with me, but I noticed that during the most troublesome times of my life there was only one set of footprints. I don't understand why, when I needed you most, you deserted me."

The Lord replied, "My precious child, I love you and would never leave you. During the times of trial and suffering, when you see only one set of footprints, those were the times when I carried you in my arms."

—Author Unknown

# SOUL PRINCIPLE

*God is always there for us, in times of joy, as well as times of sorrow or distress.*

—Dr. M. T. Morter, Jr.

**BOOSTER THOUGHT #2**
**Let it shine**

My friend, Susan, recently related this beautiful experience to me. As the mother of a twelve-year-old and a ten-year-old who had attended summer camp, she often chose to listen to the tape they had made with fellow campers the previous summer. Since the camp was a Christian-based camp, so was the music. At the time that this story took place, Susan told me that she had been a bit down. She couldn't put her finger on it, but she felt sad and lonely. Being sad didn't make sense to her, because she was happily married to wonderful man whom she loved and had two precious children who were healthy. She and her husband were also healthy. The family was financially sound. They lived in a nice home, nestled into a wooded lot in one of the most coveted neighborhoods in their area. Why was she feeling like this? What was wrong with her? And what could she do about it?

She chose the camp tape on this particular evening because most of the songs on this tape were uplifting and fun, while they also taught some good lessons. A dose of cheery, spiritual music seemed like a good antidote to the blues. However, Susan was not prepared for the eye-opening experience that occurred.

Since she was alone in her kitchen preparing dinner, she began to sing along with the songs, now committed to memory. As you know, we often sing the words to favorite songs without ever *really* hearing or feeling the words—we just blurt out the verses from rote memory, while no particular thought goes into the act. However, this evening my friend began to do more listening than singing. She said that as she truly listened to the words of the songs, she started to cry. These songs were so beautiful, so touching. The voices of the children brought tears to her eyes as she recalled her own experiences in summer camp, singing many of these same songs. She was *relating*, not only to the words of the songs, but also to the experience of camp, being with friends and counselors, and praising the Lord.

One song after another played in her kitchen that evening while Susan listened, cooked dinner, and cried. After a while, she stopped crying and started singing again, but this time with feeling, with emotion, with love. She said she couldn't remember when she had felt so good, so at peace. After the song "Let it Shine" played, she turned off the stereo to think about what had just happened to her.

She no longer felt lonely or sad. Susan now realized that she actually had everything she needed to be happy, but that she had lacked the conscious awareness to truly appreciate it. Like so many of us, Susan had begun to take her blessings for granted. She had slipped into a routine of "just going through the motions." Day after day she got up, got the kids off to school, went to work, picked up the kids, fixed dinner, watched a little TV, got the kids to bed, and fell into bed herself—only to arise the next morning and do it all again.

Susan now realized that she had blocked her spiritual self and the many blessings in her life. She had stopped "letting it shine," so she was, in essence, living in the dark. This revelation was very refreshing, once she got past the tears. Many people go through life like Susan, living in a world of darkness, when all they need to do is to let it shine. Let the spirit of the universe, the light of the world, shine through you. Open your eyes and your heart to the magnificent powers of the universe. Acknowledge the good things that exist in your own life and be thankful for your blessings. You may then get your own revelation as you let it shine and begin to resonate with the spiritual energies within you.

## SOUL PRINCIPLE

*Know that you have within you what you need to live a*
*happy, healthy, successful life.*

—Dr. M. T. Morter, Jr.

**BOOSTER THOUGHT #3**
**Is there a difference between my soul and my spirit?**

This question has been answered many times in this book. However, it is such an important concept that I felt the need to include it in the Booster Thoughts. My definition of spirit is: God, the "word," the grand plan, creative energy, innate intelligence, universal law, or any other term which means the same. The spirit is everywhere all the time. All things live according to this master plan. There is only one true, unwavering spirit. It is laser-like in intensity. The spirit of God that created us from one cell is still in and around each of us. The spiritual intelligence that took us from one cell to two cells and from two cells to four cells, is always there. That spirit has never left us.

We react to and with the spiritual information through our conscious choices. How we react to the spirit energy may separate us from the true spiritual path. The new path that we create with our conscious mind develops what I call our soul. I think it is really self explanatory in the part of the Psalm 23 that reads, "He leads me by still waters and restores my soul." Restores it to what? I believe this refers to restoring the soul back to the purity of spirit that created us in the first place.

The spirit is God's wisdom. The soul is man's logic. Man's knowledge or logic does not come close to comparing with God's wisdom. Every thought, word, and deed that man has should not interfere with the spirit (which is God's word) but should enhance it. If your actions and thoughts are in harmony with the spirit, then you are on the spiritual path. Truly living in this harmony is the ultimate goal in life. When one is on the spiritual path everything seems to go right.

## SOUL PRINCIPLE

*The spirit is godly; the soul is manly.*
—Dr. M. T. Morter, Jr.

**BOOSTER THOUGHT #4**
**What happens to my soul and my spirit when I die?**

This is a very important question. As I see it, both your soul and your spirit are made up of energy, and both the soul energy and the spirit energy leave the body when one dies. In fact, studies have been performed in which people were weighed prior to and just after death. It was found that people weigh less instantly after death than just minutes before death. So your soul and your spirit have a certain mass, a certain energy, a certain physicalness. They both leave your body and go into the universal consciousness. Sadly enough, man's contribution most often does not contain a higher level of spiritual consciousness. Generally speaking, mankind does not acknowledge the full powers of God's energy. Thus, man's contribution to the universal consciousness is more of a distraction than an amplification.

The beautiful part of the grand plan is that we have the potential to open up to the almighty power. Becoming fully aware of and believing completely in this omnipotent power can actually lead you to an inner peace and sense of contentment. Once you reach this higher level of consciousness, then you are on what I call the spiritual path. Then, when you die, your soul and spirit will leave your body as one mass of energy, not two separate masses. For me, this is the ultimate destiny. It is my desire that this will also become your destiny.

## SOUL PRINCIPLE

*When you die, your soul and spirit leave your physical body and return to the universal pool of energy.*
—Dr. M. T. Morter, Jr.

# Thoughts on Universal, Spiritual Connections

### BOOSTER THOUGHT #1
### Where is my spirit?

Although the spirit has been addressed throughout this book, I want you to have a clear understanding of the concept of spirit. Your spirit is outside of your body, inside of your body, and all around you. Your spirit envelopes every particle of your body, thus it encapsulates your entire being. It *is* the energy and information of the grand plan, or master program, and it is everywhere all the time.

The spirit or spiritual information is like a pool of water. When you jump into a pool you are immersed in the water. Think of the spirit encasing you as water does. But you need to take it one step further. This spiritual pool even envelops every atom and cell within your body. It is like a hologram. No matter how small you break it down, the whole of creation is in the smallest particle. So your spirit, which contains all the information from creation, is in and around every electron, quark, atom, and proton of your body. It is throughout your body and emanates from your body. Furthermore, spiritual information can never be altered by man or by any other physical entity. It is complete, unchanging, and everlasting.

Where is your spirit? It is in you and around you and in everything else in the universe. As I said earlier, the spirit is the universal intelligence, the grand plan, the master program, or innate wisdom. It is the all-knowing, everlasting, omnipotent knowledge that created the heavens and the earth and all things, living or non-living. Your spirit is my spirit. Our spirits are shared by all and have always been shared by all. Our spiritual being has been around forever and will always be. The spirit is an energy wave that has flowed throughout time and will continue to flow forever.

There is only one spiritual consciousness or intelligence. It is called by many different names, but it is the same spirit. Different religions and cultures have labeled this spiritual intelligence over thousands of years, but it has never changed in scope. It has always been and will always remain the same. Carl Jung said, "Whether you call the principle of existence 'God,' 'Matter,' 'Energy' or anything else you like, you have created nothing; you have simply changed a symbol."[24]

The ultimate goal or destiny of humankind is to be as one in soul and spirit. To have your soul, which is created by your conscious mind, in harmony with the spirit is the epitome of "the good life." I envision this as walking hand in hand with God.

# SOUL PRINCIPLE

*Your spirit is God, and is everywhere, all the time.*

—Dr. M. T. Morter, Jr.

## BOOSTER THOUGHT #2
### Where is God?

God is simply everywhere, all the time. He is all-knowing and perfect. This leads to the reasoning that if he is everywhere, then there is *nowhere* that God is not. So when you think about disease, you have to understand that He is there, too. He is in cancer, Hodgkin's disease, Parkinson's disease, and every other disease. Each disease is perfect—a perfect expression of survival. The question is why did you develop the disease? Not "what is it? How can I treat the symptoms? How long will it last?" but what *caused* this disease. What did I do to allow this perfect response for survival? How did I get my vitality and energy so low that this response was necessary?

One of the key elements of my way of thinking is that nothing external causes disease and nothing external can cure disease. The causes, as well as the cures, are internal—inside of each of us. Deviating from the perfect spiritual power of creation is what causes diseases and discomforts, physically and mentally. I do not believe that God intended for mankind to get diseases. It was not in the grand plan for us to be sick. We, mankind, created the necessity for diseases by deviating from the perfect, spiritual path of righteousness. Whatever condition you are in today, it is the perfect response to your soul's energy and commitment. Your current condition is the result of the choices you have made and the energy you have created. No matter what state of health you are in, it is the perfect response by the perfect power to what you have created in your energy field. It is only by returning to the spiritual path that we can eliminate the need for disease, discomfort, and illness.

Where is God? Everywhere. In health and sickness. In perfect, green, healthy trees, as well as in gnarled and diseased ones. He is in the ebb and flow of the ocean and the stillness of a fresh fallen snow. He is in the neighbor who visits your elderly mother and in the teachers who nurture and guide our children. God is in each act of kindness. He's in the tender-loving face of every newborn child. He is in the gravity that holds our world together and the process of photosynthesis, which provides the oxygen we breathe. God is within each of us and he immerses every soul. He is omniscient, omnipotent, and omnificent. Religions vary in the views they hold about God (or whatever term they use to describe the almighty power). Christians believe the kingdom of heaven is within the person. Buddhists say to look within, that you are the Buddha. The Islamic believe that those who know themselves know their God. In the Vedanta sect of Hinduism they believe that Atman, the individual consciousness, and Brahman, the universal consciousness, are one. Confucianists believe that heaven, earth, and human are of one body. Those who practice yoga, which is a part of Hinduism, believe that God dwells within you as you. Another part of Hinduism, the Upanishads, think that by understanding the self, all of the universe is known.

So, you see, views on God vary, but overall it is taught to look within oneself. Seek strength and inner awareness to manage anything that comes your way. Be thankful for all that you have, while focusing on attaining all that you want. Seek guidance and strength from his vital force so you can stay connected to the spiritual path in order to lead the epitome of a happy, healthy, and successful life.

## SOUL PRINCIPLE

*God is in all living things, throughout creation.*
—Dr. M. T. Morter, Jr.

### BOOSTER THOUGHT #3
### Universal pool of information

There is a universal consciousness, a store of knowledge common to the entire universe. This consciousness is the combination of human intellect (soul) and spiritual information (God). The human intellect provides a unique energy and awareness, thus making an important contribution to the universal consciousness. Every thought any man has ever had has contributed to the universal consciousness. Perfect spiritual information has, of course, always been there. Think of universal consciousness as an invisible pool of information that is floating around you all the time.

This pool of knowledge is available for man to withdraw information. And, on the other hand, as we think and act, we add to this pool of knowledge. So we are constantly taking from and adding to the universal consciousness. There is good, positive information in this pool, as well as negative. You can attract whatever type of information you want. In fact, in this realm, likes attract. If you put out positive vibes, you get positive feedback. When you generate negativity, you get negativity in return. Remember, not only is man's information in this pool, but, more importantly, the information from the almighty spirit is contained in this universal consciousness.

Have you ever heard the saying, "There's no such thing as a new thought?" Well, universal consciousness explains why. How about this: Have you ever wondered why you can hear a joke at home in Ohio, travel to California, and hear the same joke? And, let me add that this was true even before air travel and the internet were commonplace. Information is in the universal consciousness. Many studies have proven the concepts of universal consciousness. Studies on plants and animals have demonstrated an elaborate sensitivity and stimulus-response behavior among a variety of species. One such test was performed by Wouter van Hoven, a professor at the University of Pretoria in South Africa.[25] His study involved the *kudu*, a large spiral-horned antelope, and the trees they feed upon. During a drought, the kudu were dying. Post mortem study showed that the kudu had sufficient food in their stomachs to have kept them alive. So, van Hoven did further study on the leaves found in the stomachs of the dead kudus. He found a high tannin level in the leaves. This high level of tannin is produced by the trees when excessively irritated. In fact, study revealed that trees will begin to produce a high level of tannin after a kudu eats from its branches for only a few minutes. This explained why the kudu would eat from one tree for only a few minutes and then move on to the next, even though there were still perfectly good leaves on the first tree. It appears that it is the natural defense of the tree to produce the tannins.

The kudu is not a gentle feeder. They strip bark, and sometimes branches, while eating. So, van Hoven wondered if he could cause the trees to produce the higher tannin levels by mistreating the trees. First, he tiptoed up to the tree and took a few sample leaves. Then, he and a team of students imitated the feeding process of the kudu by beating the trees with belts, whips, and canes. He then took more leaf samples. He found that the leaves of the trees had a higher tannin level after being mistreated. But even more interesting, nearby plants also showed a marked increase in tannin production. These undamaged plants could be as far as ten feet away from the mistreated plant. They simply responded to the mistreated trees, perhaps in self-preservation or possibly sympathetically. Who knows, but they did react. This, again, shows the universal consciousness. The nearby, but undamaged, trees responded to information in the energy field around them.

Other scientists have revealed similar findings that have led to the belief that airborne pheromonal substances may be responsible for this plant-to-plant communication. Pheromones, chemicals produced by animals to serve as a stimulus to other animals of the same species, had previously been considered specific to the animal kingdom. Some believe that chemical communication is also responsible for the communication between plants. Many studies have now proven that there is even universal communication at the subconscious level.

Here are a couple of great examples of this type of communication between animals and their owners. In his book *Beyond Supernature,* Lyall Watson reports these two interesting cases recorded by psychologist Michael Fox of Washington University:

> "... two cases of traveling cats that could be recognised by distinctive marks. One belonged to a New York veterinarian who left his pet behind when going to take up a new post 2,500 miles away in California. Some months later, an identical cat walked into his new home. Incredulously, he examined the animal and found a deformation on the fourth vertebra of the tail—an injury he had himself treated when the cat was bitten as a kitten. The second restless cat was a Persian

called Smoky, distinguished by a tuft of reddish hair beneath his chin. Smoky leaped from a window of the family car when its owners were in the process of moving house. Neighbours near the old home in Oklahoma said the cat was prowling around there for several days, but a year later it turned up 300 miles away at the family's new and totally unfamiliar home in Tennessee."[26]

J. B. Rhine at Duke University has gathered a collection of fifty-four spontaneous cases in which "an animal, separated from a mate or owner, followed it into wholly unfamiliar territory under conditions that preclude the use of a sensory trail."[27] This subconscious communication among plants and animals and man is all in the name of survival and all according to the grand plan, spiritual information, and universal consciousness.

When the human consciousness, or soul, leaves the body when we die, the information from the soul then contributes to God's wisdom to add to the pool of universal consciousness. Mankind is only a tiny piece in the giant puzzle of life— a comma in the almanac of history.

## SOUL PRINCIPLE

*The universal pool of information, or universal consciousness, created and runs the entire universe.*
                                                —Dr. M. T. Morter, Jr.

# Thoughts on Believing in Your Perfect Self

### BOOSTER THOUGHT #1
### What do Christians mean when they say, "Jesus is my savior"?

This is a warm, fuzzy thought. It feels good for many people. However, let's evaluate what this statement really means. If you are not a Christian, but a follower of some other religion, then you may insert the name for your deity in the place of Jesus throughout this section. First, let's examine what *you* believe. If you believe "Jesus is my savior" *and* Jesus is "out there somewhere," then you are believing that someone "out there" is going to save you. Does this make sense? Is it wise to think that someone "out there" is going to save you? You see, I don't believe that Jesus is "out there" somewhere. I also don't believe he will save me if I'm drowning or pay my debts when I overspend. I don't think he will keep me out of prison if I steal. I do not believe that someone "out there" is my savior "in here." In my opinion, Jesus is *inside* of each of us. It is his power within us that will save us. Following his teachings and the examples he set will save us. Connecting with the spiritual path will save us.

Jesus came here to teach us how to be saved by following his example, he came here to teach us how to save ourselves. That is completely different from something "out there" saving us. It takes it to an internal concept of "I can save myself by acknowledging the truth, the light, the word. I can save myself by following the spiritual path." Jesus Christ said, "The kingdom of God, of heaven, is within you." Think about what "Jesus is my savior" means to you. Is Jesus somewhere "out there" or is he *inside* of you?

## SOUL PRINCIPLE

*The spirit of Jesus is within you.*

—Dr. M. T. Morter, Jr.

### BOOSTER THOUGHT #2
#### Has my savior arrived on earth yet?

Some people do not believe that their "savior" has arrived on earth yet. They believe that someone else is going to come, not Jesus, to show us the way. How many times do we need to be shown the way? In my opinion Jesus was sent as an example. He was sent to show us the spiritual path. Jesus taught us God's word. The word is, was, and will always be the same. It is perfect; it is unwavering. Our ultimate goal is to acknowledge, accept, and live by the word. Our free will to choose to eat certain foods, smoke or not, stay up late or go to bed early are secondary choices. The primary choice of free will is whether or not you acknowledge the one ultimate power. It doesn't matter if Jesus is your role model, your savior, or if someone else fills that position. What matters is that you identify, acknowledge, accept, and live by the one true power. That power I call God.

## SOUL PRINCIPLE

*The word of God is our savior.*

—Dr. M. T. Morter, Jr.

**BOOSTER THOUGHT #3**
**Chakras**

There are seven *chakras* of the body. All the energy of your body runs between these energy points or *chakras*. They begin at the base of the spine and run to the crown of the head. The chakras are identified with the colors of the spectrum of light. The first chakra, at the base of the spine, is the color red. The second chakra is at the sacral (or bottom) vertebrae, with the color orange. The solar plexus, which is in the pit of the stomach, is the third chakra and its color is yellow. Number four is at the heart and is green. The fifth chakra, at the throat, is blue. The head is the sixth chakra and its color is indigo. The seventh chakra, the crown chakra, is violet or blue-white. There is a channel of energy flowing between these chakras within you. This passageway is visible to those who meditate on it. Each of you is capable of seeing your own chakra points by actually seeing the color of that point.

Man has always been interested in studying where he came from and his purpose in life. The world within people has been studied for thousands of years. It is through meditation that you can reach your inner world, your higher level of consciousness. Sound is often associated with meditation, as certain combinations of sounds are considered innately powerful in the ability to reach the spirit or God-force within us. It was over two thousand years ago that Patanjali established the yoga *sutras*, which are still followed by many today. These sutras were developed for the purpose of leading people to the highest state of consciousness.

This sublime state of awareness is known as the siddhi conscious-ness. He taught his students to meditate by repeating the sound *Aum*. Patanjali also taught that repetition of this sound would relieve the mind of obstacles and arouse the student's mind to a new, higher level of consciousness. Many spiritual teachers today continue to follow these practices.

Some teach to use the *aaah* sound, as well as the *om* or *aum* sound. The *aaah* sound is believed to be contained in the name for the divine creator in all Eastern and Western religions, primitive societies, and other traditions or cultures. It is the sound of perfection—the sound of God, the sound of joy, the sound of creation. The *aaah* sound in meditation is used to integrate with the spiritual energy and emit an energy of unconditional love into the universe. Those who practice manifestation believe that it is through meditating with this sound and projecting through the use of chakras that they are able to manifest, or create, the objects of their desire. Most spiritual leaders recommend using the *aaah* sound in the morning meditation session, as the new day is unfolding. The silence of this time of day coupled with the almighty energy of the sunrise are believed to enhance the power of the meditation. Sit comfortably, outdoors if possible, and re-peat the *aaah* sound over and over. While you do this, focus on what it is that you wish to bring into your life. Think of how you will *feel* when this is brought to you. It is not necessary to decide *how* this will happen, only how you feel.

The *om* sound is felt to be the sound of that which has al-ready been created. It is the sound associated with vibrational frequencies in the physical plane. It is said that women in an-cient times repeated this sound while birthing babies. *Om* is used to convey thankfulness or gratitude. Using this sound will con-nect you to your life, to your environment, and to the spirit. This meditation sound is used at sunset. Meditate, in a comfortable position, using the *om* sound as the sun goes down. (Again, if you can be outdoors, it is even better.) As you repeat the sound, be thankful for all that you have, for the world around you, na-ture, and humanity. The feeling of gratitude that accompanies this practice is all-encompassing. You will feel the power of the universe surging within you.

Another wonderful meditation is done indoors in a dark room. Sit comfortably, close your eyes, and look for colors. You may use the *aaah* sound to clear your mind as you do this exercise. You will begin to see colors develop. The colors you see will tell you with which part of your soul you are vibrating. The ultimate in this experience is to see violet or blue-white. We each have the ability to develop this visual, but it may take some time to do so.

For instance, if you see red (the color of the base chakra), your energy is blocked at the spine. Remember, your energy flows from the first chakra, at the base of the spine, to the seventh chakra, at the crown. The color you see indicates a sort of blockage in your physical body.

You may see yellow or green. Keep asking or meditating to see the color violet, as the ability to see and maintain a visual of the color violet is the goal of this meditation. It is important to be thankful that you are in communication as soon as you see any color. You are now aware of your soul frequency. This is a way to evaluate where you are on the soul level. Be thankful for the color you see, and then ask for the next color up. Be patient. You may not see the next color in that session. In fact, it may be several or many sessions before you are able to move up to the next color. That is all right and quite normal. The point is, eventually you will be able to see violet or blue-white.

When I first could see this, it was a fleeting color. It wouldn't stay. I would try to catch it and hold it, but I was unable to do so. I now can get this color and I can hold it for as long as I want to meditate with it. The feeling you will attain as you reach this level of consciousness is one of complete harmony—a feeling of belonging, not controlling. This congruent, harmonic state aligns your soul with your spirit and opens the way for direct contact with the divine creator. This is a journey *everyone* can take. It is a journey of cause, creation, and soul–spirit unity. I encourage you to practice all of these mantras in your search for the divine connection.

## SOUL PRINCIPLE

*Meditation can take you to a higher level of consciousness.*
—Dr. M. T. Morter, Jr.

# Dr. Morter's Belief Builders
### PRESCRIPTIONS FOR THE SPIRITUAL PLANE

- I have the power of the universe within me, waiting for my direction.
- My happiness depends on me.
- My communion with the spiritual energy of creation (God) is my personal path of fulfillment.
- My spiritual field controls my physical body.
- The positive information in my spiritual field attracts positivity to me.
- Being neutral is not enough to promote health; I must be positive.
- My relationships are an expression of what is in my field.
- My goal is to have my soul and my spirit resonate harmoniously.
- People can't hear what I say if who I *am* is relaying a different message.
- Praying with gratitude and thankfulness is positive prayer.
- It would be a highly successful life if everyone I met from the time I was born until the time I died was glad to have met me.
- I won't give *up*, I will give *in* to God's unconditional love.
- I can neutralize negative events in my life by blanketing them with positive thoughts and feelings.
- I can harvest the energy of my field.
- I can change my life by tapping into the creative, universal energy within me.

- The knowledge and wisdom of all time is available to me in the universal consciousness.
- To *know* is to be certain beyond doubt.
- I can and do bring into existence the things that I think about.
- I can convert my dreams into realities.
- All living systems use creative energy.
- The universal energy resides within us at all times.
- The part of me that runs my body does not think, judge, or reason.
- I will see it, when I believe it.
- I will practice the three steps of forgiveness daily.

PART III

# The Path
# of Fulfillment

A well cultivated mind is made up of all
the minds of preceding ages; it is only the
one single mind educated by all previous
time.

—Bernard le Bovier de Fontenelle

CHAPTER 6

# Universal Consciousness

**The end of life is to be like God, and the soul
following God will be like him.**
—Socrates

Universal consciousness is a combination of the energy of
your soul and the silent language of the almighty spiritual power.
It is unspoken, yet accessible by every living entity in the entire
universe. It is not a different language for different people, but
one common energy shared by all—humans, animals, trees, grass,
bacteria, plankton, and every living thing. It is the thread that
binds the universe. Universal consciousness is a pool of energy,
information, and power that is unseen, but highly visible in every facet of creation.

## Original Spirit

As you know, I call the owner of the ultimate universal power
God. And I believe that God is in control. He is the voice of universal consciousness. He is the *original* spirit, the origin and
source from which everything arose. God is the master spirit or
energy from which all copies are made. Man's goal in life is to
reproduce from this master, this original, to try to copy this original as closely as possible. God's energy and power envelope the
universe in a constant fashion, encapsulating and penetrating
every being so that we are not only surrounded by the universal
consciousness, but it is also within us.

We, like the trees, just respond to this information. For example, when you plant a seed, it grows. All of the information of the universal consciousness is inside of the seed. It knows what to do. It knows what nutrients to take from the soil, how to sprout, what to become, and it just does that. You have nothing to do with what each seed will grow into being. You only plant it in soil and water it occasionally. The seed does all the work. It has all the knowledge within it to become what it is destined to become.

This innate information comes to the universe in a variety of ways. One way that is easily observed is pulsing waves. I recently observed the pulse of a huge tank of jellyfish. At an aquarium, I stood and watched the pulsation of individual jellyfish. After some time, I noticed that they were all pulsating at the same time. Each jellyfish, and thus the entire mass of jellyfish, pulsed in synchronization. It is this pulse, or wave, that is apparent in the ocean tides. It is also this pulse that I feel when I work to synchronize the bodies of my patients. It's the pulse of life, the universal pulse. It bombards the universe and it just is.

The original spirit is responsible for turning the acorn into the mighty oak, and the egg into the chick. It makes grass green and the ocean blue. It creates oxygen for us to breathe. The human life begins with the pulse, which can be seen in the tiny embryo. This universal consciousness affects everything all the time.

One example of the omnipresence of the original spirit is the heart beat. A heart, taken out of the body, will beat about forty-eight beats per minute. When inside the body, the heartbeat is increased to about seventy-two beats per minute. The heart responds to the universal information, all the time. You know that it is not under conscious control, because it continues to beat while you sleep. The universal intelligence never rests, it is perpetual and constant.

# Differentiation of Spirit and Soul

We each respond to the universal consciousness from the moment of our conception. As a fetus, we are enveloped by this spiritual consciousness as well as by our mother's energy field.

Remember, our mother's field is her interpretation of and adaptation to the spiritual consciousness—her soul. As we grow and develop, we each create our own soul or field. So we have the spiritual consciousness within us and our own soul within us. They both surround us, as well. Our soul, which we create, is our adaptation of knowledge and feeling toward the world around us. While we listen, learn, develop, and grow, we actually create our own unique soul, and our soul contributes to the universal consciousness. The pool of energy in and around us is a combination of the divine, spiritual consciousness and our own soul.

If your knowledge and feelings are congruent with the spiritual knowledge or consciousness, then your spirit and soul are harmonious. However, if you begin to develop feelings of hate, anger, jealousy, fear, and the like, then you are separating yourself from the spiritual consciousness. You are building barriers between yourself and God's energy. Nothing you do ever affects that universal power, but it may serve to isolate you from it. Remember, God never turns his back on us. Rather, we sometimes turn our backs on him.

Living under the influence of a negative soul can and will contaminate your body. Disease and ill-health result when the energy of your soul is allowed to run in a negative manner. All of the negative emotions that you harbor vent themselves by polluting your health. In other words, negative feelings create a negative soul, which manifests in poor health. This state of being is not in perfect communication with the divine universal consciousness. In fact, it is in direct opposition to this information or energy. It is this misalignment that causes ill-health and disease. So you see, disease is a perfect positive response to negative soul energy.

The development of man's soul is depicted from the beginning of recorded time. Christians believe that when Adam and Eve ate the apple from the forbidden tree, they were choosing to use their free wills to satisfy themselves. Even though they had been warned not to eat this fruit, they chose to do so anyway. This is an example of man developing a consciousness that is contrary to the one true spiritual consciousness. This act served to isolate Adam and Eve from God. They were separated from his way, just as we are today when we choose not to follow the divine path he has laid out for us. We all repeat daily the same sins of Adam and Eve. We continue to miss the mark.

So, when you live with a negative soul, you separate yourself from the divine spiritual path. That path is still there, you are just not on it. Our saving grace is that we have pure, spiritual, universal consciousness available to us at all times. It is always present, everywhere, at all times. All we have to do is open our hearts and souls to allow it into our personal consciousness. We have the option to do this at any time. Right now, this minute, you can decide to change your soul's path and turn it back toward the divine path of the universal consciousness. Your decisions, which create your soul, can strengthen your bond with God or break it. The choice is yours. The development of your soul is a personal endeavor, one which only you endure.

When your soul is in alignment with the spiritual path you will feel a calmness, a sense of peace. It is written in Psalm 23:

## SOUL PRINCIPLE

*The Lord is my shepherd, I shall not be in want. He makes me lie down in green pastures, he leads me beside quiet waters, he restores my soul. He guides me in paths of righteousness for his name's sake. Even though I walk through the valley of the shadow of death, I will fear no evil, for you are with me; your rod and your staff, they comfort me.*

—Psalm 23:1–6

When you are in tune with the spiritual consciousness, (God) then you walk by calm waters, you lie in green pastures. When you are faced with frightening challenges, you will not be afraid. He will restore your soul. When you stay on the path of righteousness, you will be comforted by the spirit within you.

# Man's Contribution to Universal Consciousness

Here's an analogy to depict the relationship between the energies of the soul and spirit. The spiritual energy is white in color—pure, perfect, ethereal, and white. On the other hand, when you use your conscious mind to make negative choices that lead you away from the spiritual path, then the color of your energy is black. Since these energies combine to envelop you, the energy surrounding you is some shade of gray—the combination of white and black. This is your energy field. This mixture of gray energy that surrounds us all the time is actually made up of distinct particles of both white and black.

With your free will you make decisions. Each decision you make resonates with the black energy or the white energy of your field. When your thoughts, actions, and deeds are harmonious with the spiritual path, then you attract more of the white energy to you. You resonate and pulsate with this white energy. The more white energy you attract, the happier and healthier you become. You walk by calm waters, you do not fear. Your life becomes an attracting field of good and positive events and the course of your soul and spirit are synchronized. You emit and attract white energy. You will have a feeling of everything going your way on these days.

If you make poor decisions, are depressed, scared, lonely, and angry, then you will attract the black energy particles from your field of energy. This black energy will attract more black energy. You will resonate in a pool of black energy, becoming more depressed, more unhealthy, or more diseased. When you go to the doctor and he tells you that you have fibromyalgia, that is the same to me as saying that you are attracting black energy or information. Why are you attracting this? Because that is what you are emitting by your thoughts, actions, and deeds. What you put out into the world, you will get back. As you give, so shall you receive—even tenfold.

When you die, the energy from your soul and your spirit will leave your physical body and return to the universal pool of consciousness. The thoughts and acts of your entire lifetime will be dispersed into the pool of universal consciousness, joining with the pure white contribution of the divine spirit. Just as you have the opportunity to take from this universal pool, so do you contribute to it.

## SOUL PRINCIPLE

*Every generation enjoys the use of a vast hoard bequeathed to it by antiquity, and transmits that hoard, augmented by fresh acquisitions, to the future ages.*
—Thomas Babington Macaulay

It is your choice what contribution you will make to the universal pool of consciousness. Will you add a great clutter of black energy? Or will you increase the resonance of the white energy? Only you can determine the size of the ripple you will make in this great pool. Your contribution to the universal consciousness is not measured or judged, it just is what it is. Just as surely as night follows day, you will make a splash in this pool of knowledge, energy, and power. You can decide now to brighten your energy, growing ever nearer to that divine, ethereal white energy. The beauty of it all is that you have the ability to choose your path and to choose the quality of the contribution you make to the universal consciousness. You can thank God for this freedom and this power.

CHAPTER 7

# Practical Steps
# to a Healthy Life

Be such a man, and live such a life, that if every
man were such as you, and every life a life like
yours, this earth would be God's Paradise.
—Phillips Brooks

By now you should have a good understanding of my principles. This chapter is devoted to helping you utilize these principles in your daily life. Any theology, philosophy, concept, or
principle is only credible and useful to mankind if it may actually
be applied on a practical basis; otherwise it may be sound in
thought, but impractical in practice. If a school of thought is
impractical, then it is viewed as "out there" and may be followed
by some, but not by the masses. The concepts I have shared with
you in this book are user friendly. They are meant to be used as
guiding lights on your path of life. I am a simple man, sharing a
simple truth.

## Your Health Is Up to You

In Part I, the Six Essentials for Life were outlined and explained. It is important to understand that I view these six elements as the essential, vital facets of your life. I feel that your
choices in these six areas are critical to your well being and your
overall health. As review, the Six Essentials for Life are:

What you eat
What you drink
How you exercise
How you rest
What you breathe
What you think

Making proper choices in these six areas of your life will strengthen your body, your mind, and your soul. Remember, the more good choices you make, the closer you will be to walking in alignment with the perfect spiritual path, which is, in the end, our ultimate goal. To be in tune with our spirit—God's spirit—is the epitome of the good life. And this is only possible when you take care of yourself and make the right choices in *every* facet of your life. You may attend church, temple, or synagogue at every opportunity, but if you don't live your daily life according to God's plan, then you may be no closer to walking in tune with your spirit than someone who never darkens the doorstep of a house of worship. If you exercise like a fitness fiend but only eat junk food, then you, too, are off the path. If you eat the right foods and exercise regularly, but work in a chemically polluted environment breathing in toxic wastes eight hours per day, then your road to health is also askew. In other words, it is a combination of overall good choices in *every one* of the six essentials that leads to excellent health and well-being—the spiritual path of fulfillment.

When it comes to your diet, whose choice is it? Is it your mother's choice? Your wife's or your husband's? Could it be your cook's choice? Or is it your own? I mean, really, who decides what food you put in your mouth? *You do.* You choose what you eat as well as what you drink. Rare are the cases that involve someone having their diet mandated. The vast majority of us are at liberty to eat and drink exactly what we choose. In Chapter 3 there is a table of foods that are the best choices for you if you want to maintain a balanced diet. The best drink choice is pure water that has been filtered by the reverse osmosis method. Don't be fooled into believing that wine or any other alcoholic beverage is good for you. Take charge of your life and you will be relaxed without alcohol or other stimulants. Choose well.

## SOUL PRINCIPLE

*If the mind, that rules the body, ever so far forgets itself as to trample on its slave, the slave is never generous enough to forgive the injury, but will rise and smite the oppressor.*
—Henry Wadsworth Longfellow

This freedom to choose carries over into our exercise regimens or lack thereof. Do you call exercise walking to your car in the morning or going out to get the mail at the end of your driveway? Is it exercise when you walk to the refrigerator to get the ice cream? Can you really call it exercise when you walk upstairs to get in bed? Not many of you answered yes, I hope. Remember, exercise should be regular and fun.

Choose a form of exercise that you enjoy. Walking is a great way to get some exercise, while it also allows for time to think some happy thoughts, evaluate your intentions, or visit with a loved one. If you enjoy swimming, then make that your regular exercise outlet. You may want or need to join an exercise class or a fully-equipped gym. Some people find they are more motivated when working out with others. Some even prefer a personal trainer who holds them accountable for reaching fitness goals. You may enjoy riding a bicycle or roller skating. Or you may like to vary your form of exercise: swimming on Monday, walking on Wednesday, and riding your bike on Friday. Whatever form of exercise you choose, do it on a regular basis. Regular basis means thirty minutes to an hour, three to four times a week. Enjoy your exercise. View your ability to exercise as a celebration of your health and your life. Do it with a smile on your face and in your heart. It will make the experience more fulfilling and more fun.

As far as your freedom goes, it also applies to how much rest you get. If you are in your teen to adult years, then you probably have a good idea of how much sleep you need in order to feel rested, energetic, and alert. Don't kid yourself by thinking you can get by with less—it just doesn't work. Eventually your body will break down and demand that you rest. It may come in the form of an illness, a disease, or a broken bone, but your body will become exhausted in some way. At that point, you will be forced to rest. Perhaps you can see the logic in getting the rest you need *prior* to becoming ill. I surely hope so. Remember, there is a difference between sleep and rest. If you sleep under the influence of a drug, then your body is not getting the rest it needs because it is forced to react to the chemicals. There are also side effects. These unpleasant side effects are natural reactions carried out by your perfect, subconscious mind. No choice, no thought, no judgment, just reaction.

Sleeping while in defensive physiology is also not restful. Defense physiology is produced when you go to bed uptight, tense, and worried about something or everything. You actually go to sleep and super glue these feelings into your physiology; they are imprinted on your hard drive. This puts you into subconscious emotional memory override.

Here's a simple test. As you are reading this book, right now, can you lower your shoulders when you consciously think of it? If you can, your body was functioning under subconscious emotional memory override. You are wasting energy, right now, just as though you are frightened by a bear. Living in a state of emotional memory override is not restful. So, you must deal with your feelings and emotions while you are awake. Confront your situations in order to overcome them. When you go to bed at night, review the good things that happened to you that day. Be thankful for the blessings in your life. See the good in the experiences you have had, in order to learn the lessons. Then you can go to sleep in a state of peacefulness by taking a few deep breaths and floating off into a pleasant dream.

While we are discussing deep breaths, let's review the fifth essential for life, what you breathe. This is the one that you just can't put off until later. You simply have to breathe. Sure you can play with your breathing techniques, but you simply must breathe. The key here is to breathe clean, pure, healthy air, not chemical-laden, toxic waste. Do not breathe a nicotine-enhanced climate or a smog-ridden, polluted environment. Just good old clean air—Mother Nature's freebie. This sounds simple enough, but if you live or work in a polluted area, then you may have some serious health choices to make. Just how detrimental is the situation you are in? Can you compensate by making near-perfect choices in the other six essentials? Or do you need to change jobs or move in order to improve your health status? Maybe you need to quit smoking or address someone else's smoking habits. Ultimately, the decision about what you breathe is up to you. Evaluate your surroundings, determine the quality of the air you breathe, and adjust your life accordingly.

## SOUL PRINCIPLE

*The main purpose of life is to live rightly, think rightly, act rightly; the soul must languish when we give all our thoughts to the body.*

—Mahatma Gandhi

This leads us to the last, but not least, essential for life: what you think. As I have stated, your thinking is the most important of the six essentials. What you think determines who you are. What you thought in the past determined who you are today. What you think today determines who you will become in the future. Let me repeat that, *what you think today determines who you will become in the future.* The past is just that—past. It is behind you. Learn from your past experiences and then leave them behind you. As you live new experiences, learn from them *as* you encounter them.

Learning the lessons from your past, and current, situations will allow you to see the good in the experiences. Once you have established *why* you experienced something then you will be able to move on in a healthy frame of mind. Remember, there is *always* something good in a situation. You may have a little difficulty discovering goodness in a given situation, but be assured that it is there. Dig deep and find the good in it for *you*. Why are you better today for having experienced this? You may only be able to determine that you would never treat someone a certain way or that you are stronger for having lived through a particular event. You may realize that you are now equipped to help others in similar situations. Some of the most respected philanthropists, speakers, entrepreneurs, and theologians rose to their great heights by recognizing the good in unpleasant, if not awful, situations in their personal lives and overcoming those situations by learning the lessons they offered and actually putting them to use as motivating forces in their lives. You, too, can turn seemingly terrible experiences into enlightening opportunities. Don't view these experiences as problems, but rather see them as areas to learn from, to gain strength from, to overcome. Use them as stepping stones to a higher level of consciousness—or as stepping stones on your path of fulfillment.

# A New Definition of Preventative Medicine

Here's a new way of looking at preventative medicine. First, let's explore the definition of medicine. Webster defines medicine as: "1) a: a substance or preparation used in treating disease, b: something that affects well-being; 2) a: the science and art dealing with the maintenance of health and the prevention, alleviation, or cure of disease, b: the branch of medicine concerned with the nonsurgical treatment of disease."

I especially like definition number two and feel that we are all capable of dealing with the art of maintenance, prevention, alleviation, and, yes, even *cure*, of disease. First, maintenance of health is what life is all about. Making good choices in the Six Essentials For Life is directly linked to attaining and maintaining good health.

## SOUL PRINCIPLE

*Who would not give a trifle to prevent what he would give a thousand worlds to cure?*

—Edward Young

Now, here's a new way of looking at prevention: make changes *before* symptoms occur and disease develops. Evaluate your life and your lifestyle. Put yourself under an imaginary microscope, probe into every area of your life to determine where you are performing well and where you have room for improvement. Perform this simple, general evaluation to see how you score.

Take out a pencil and a pad of paper. Make a heading for each of the Six Essentials for Life. Now, under each heading, truthfully fill in the answers from your daily life. Give yourself one week to adequately determine these answers. 1) Write down *everything* you eat and drink for one week. At the end of each day, determine the percentage of your diet that came from the alkaline food list and the percentage that derived from the acid food list (see Chapter 3). Alcoholic beverages do not appear on the food list, but they have an acidifying affect on the body. 2) Document the number of minutes or hours that you exercise each day. 3) Write down the number of hours you sleep each day and night for one week. Rate how well you rested on a scale of one to five, with one representing poorly and five representing very well. 4) Evaluate the air you breathe each day using a scale from one to five, with one representing totally polluted, toxic, smoke-filled, or smog-ridden air and five representing good, clean air. 5) Lastly, evaluate your thinking each day. Again, use a scale of one to five. Let one represent a day of the gloomiest, saddest, most depressing and negative thoughts and let five represent a day of the purest, happiest, most positive thoughts.

By the end of one week you should be able to determine how well you score in the Six Essentials for Life. A quick analysis of the numbers will tell you how you rated. Here's a general overview of how to score your results.

- **What you eat and drink**—The general rule of thumb here is that your diet should consist of seventy-five percent fruits and vegetables. Pure, one-hundred percent fruit and vegetable juices fall into this category. The perfect drink is pure water. Anything other than pure water or pure fruit or vegetable juice is acidic. The remaining twenty-five percent of your diet includes everything else you consume. So, you can evaluate your percentage each day according to the ideal seventy-five/ twenty-five percent guideline. The closer you are to seventy-five percent alkaline food, the better your score.

- **How you exercise**—The basic rule in this area is to exercise thirty minutes to an hour, three to four days per week. You may choose to do more and to set higher goals for yourself. Your exercise should meet the criteria explained in Chapter 2. Ultimately, keep moving and move in ways you enjoy!
- **How you rest**—Most experts agree that adults, in general, need eight hours of sleep per night. Resting is a different matter. You may sleep ten hours a night and wake up as tired as when you went to sleep. You slept, but you didn't rest. When evaluating your rest, a perfect score of five each day would result in a total score of thirty-five. Generally, a score of twenty-eight to thirty-five is very good. A score in the twenty to twenty-seven range is mediocre and could use some improvement. A score of thirteen to nineteen results when there is a need for definite improvement. And, a score of twelve and below shows a drastic need for improvement.
- **What you breathe**—This is one of the most important of the six essentials, but also one of the most objective. Only you can determine and rate the effect of the air that you breathe. Obviously, the Surgeon General of the United States, as well as your healthcare provider, can determine that cigarette smoking is harmful to your health. (I'd like to add here, that smoking *anything* is harmful to your health.) However, the environment in which you live and breathe can only be evaluated by you. According to the rating scale provided, a score of thirty-five would result when you breathed only good, clean air. A score of twenty-eight to thirty-five is a very good score. A score of twenty to twenty-seven leaves some room for improvement, while a score of nineteen and below shows a definite need for improvement.

- **What you think**—Again, what you think about on a regular basis determines who you are and your level of physical and mental health. What you think is by far the most important of the Six Essentials for Life. A perfect week in this area would result in a score of thirty-five. If you scored twenty-six to thirty-five points you had a very good week. A rating of eighteen to twenty-five indicates a good week, but leaves room for improvement, while a score of seventeen and below indicates a poor week.

This simple test of the Six Essentials for Life should give you a good indication of how you are doing in the most vital areas of your life. Be honest with your ratings and take a close look at each area. You will probably see that you really shine in some areas, while you need to make some improvements in others. Remember, it is a good balance between all of the six essential elements that leads to a healthy, happy, and successful state of being.

## SOUL PRINCIPLE

*Begin to be now what you will be hereafter.*
—Jerome (Eusebius Hieronymus)

Let's review Webster's definition of medicine: "2) a: the science and art dealing with the maintenance of health and the prevention, alleviation, or cure of disease." By working to balance and maintain higher scores in the six essential areas of your life you will be taking a step of *preventative* medicine, because you will be improving your state of health before illness or disease becomes necessary. If you are experiencing an illness or ailments of some kind, you may find that simply focusing on a balance in these six areas will serve to alleviate your health challenges. And providing your body with the highest possible levels of health in each of these six areas will actually allow your body to work, innately, to actually *cure* itself of the health challenges it is experiencing.

# Practicing the Steps of Forgiveness

In Chapter 4, the steps of forgiveness were outlined. Please refer to that section for a thorough review of the steps. Here's a quick recap.

- Step one is self-forgiveness. You must forgive yourself for any harm you may have caused yourself due to any given event in your life.
- Step two is to forgive the other person involved.
- Step three is to give the other person permission to forgive you.

Some of you may view these steps as innocuous enough, while others may feel threatened, even offended, at the thought of forgiving. Depending on the experiences of your life, you will react somewhere on a scale between eagerness and readiness to forgive, to fearfulness and hostility toward forgiving.

I want you to understand that I believe learning to forgive is one of the most important aspects of this book. I believe that *your reactions to the experiences in your life hold the answers to your state of health.* How you have responded in the past and how you respond today to the multitude of events in your life determines your state of health today and in the future. If you tend to harbor resentment, anger, jealousy, hate, and other such strong, negative emotions, then you are probably experiencing some disease in your life. I believe that every disease is an expression of an unlearned lesson. When negative emotions are held in your heart and your mind day after day, month after month, and year after year, the result can be devastating to your health, even life-threatening. Following the simple steps of forgiveness can alleviate much of the pain and fear of the experience, thus allowing for a state of ease, rather than disease.

## SOUL PRINCIPLE

*I am not afraid of storms for I am learning how to sail my ship.*

—Louisa May Alcott

The one essential key to forgiveness is *sincerity*. In order for these steps to be effective, you must perform them with feeling and emotion. You must truly mean what you say as you go through each of the steps. Your feelings of forgiveness must be as strong to the positive side as your feelings toward the event which you are forgiving are to the negative side. In other words, you must actually balance or neutralize your negative feelings toward the situation by blanketing it with positive, loving feelings. This does not mean that you must now view the situation or person as good or that you agree with or condone his actions. What it means is that you must see the good in the situation as it relates to *you*. When you can learn the lesson from the experience, then you will see the good in the experience. Finding the good in the situation has been described to me as "like flipping a switch and turning on a light." Once you see the good in the experience, then you know *why* it happened and what lesson it offers you. The good lesson may now be glaringly obvious. You may even wonder why you never recognized it before. The key is that you now see the good and learn the lesson.

As I have said before, it may be difficult to perform the steps of forgiveness at first, but you will get better at it with each experience. The toughest lessons to learn are the first ones that you tackle. Those nagging experiences from your past may have been haunting you for a long time. These situations may be hard to overcome, but I believe that your health depends on your ability to do so. As you begin to apply the steps of forgiveness to current situations, you will see how easily you can adopt the practice into your every day living. Remember, things don't happen *to* you, they happen *for* you—to learn a lesson. If you learn the lesson correctly, it will enable you to give and receive unconditional love. Be thankful for each lesson you are offered, not only those in your past, but also the lesson of the moment.

By learning from life as it unfolds, you no longer have the need to store negative experiences in memory. See the lesson in each of these experiences *now*, filling your storage bank with good memories. This will allow for peace of mind and a better state of health. Again, it's preventative medicine—preventing the need for medicine. As you handle each experience of your life by seeing the good in it and learning the lesson it has to offer, then you will begin to turn your path of life back toward the one, true path. You will take a giant step toward God's spiritual path and begin to resonate more harmoniously in soul and spirit.

# Proper Prayer— Be Thankful, Love More

It is important to remember that I believe that your physical body is controlled by your spiritual field. The spiritual field in and around you actually determines your level of health. If you put out negative thoughts and information, you will attract negativity to your life. You will actually interfere with the perfect, creative, loving spiritual field of God. You create "static" in your life. On the other hand, putting out positive thoughts and information attracts positiveness, which allows for the healthy flow between your physical body and the perfect, spiritual realm. So your physical field, or body, can be altered by what you think with your mind. However, just "not thinking negatively" (in other words, being neutral) is not enough to promote health. You must actually *be* positive. Taking a positive role, a proactive stance, can literally change your life.

One of the simplest ways to do this is through prayer. The power of prayer has been touted by many for generations. It is not necessary for me to try to explain this here, but I do want to sing the praises of prayer. Positive, healthy prayer not only makes you feel good by putting you in a peaceful state of mind, but it also serves to interface your soul and your spirit. It works to help connect you with the spiritual path. It puts you in communion with God. I believe that prayer should always be in the affirmative. It should always be positive.

## SOUL PRINCIPLE

*Prayer is the wing wherewith the soul flies to heaven, and meditation the eye wherewith we see God.*
—Ambrose of Milan

When you pray, pray with gratitude. Be thankful for all of the good things in your life. Give thanks for the perfect expression of life and spirit that flows through you. Give thanks for what you want as if you have already received it. By now we have looked backward in our lives and worked to understand, forgive, and learn from our negative past experiences. As you recall these experiences, pray with thanks for these experiences in your life. Be thankful for the lessons they have taught you. As you encounter challenging situations on a daily basis, be thankful for the lessons each experience brings. See the good in it for *you*. Each night when you pray, be thankful for the lessons of the day.

Here are some guidelines for successful, positive prayer. Keep in mind that these general precepts are meant to aid you in communicating with your spirit and walking the true spiritual path. You may already follow such principles or have a regimen that works well for you.

1.  Identify that there is an ultimate power—God, or whatever title you deem to use to describe the omnipotent force of the universe.
2.  Recognize that the force of this power resides within you, as well as around you, and further encompasses all of creation as we know it—and even beyond.
3.  Surrender to the perfect strength and might of God's power as the ultimate energy source.
4.  Know that only positive, wholesome, healthful thoughts and images are in line with God's one true spiritual path.
5.  Believe you have already achieved the specific goals you wish to achieve and be thankful for them, as if you have already received them.

6. Meditate on God's *unconditional love*; love *more* and expect *less*.
7. Be ever thankful for life—that of mankind, animals, plants, and all of God's creation.

Following these or similar principles will lead to more successful prayer. If you faithfully follow these precepts you can achieve tremendous results, changing your life forever. The powers of forgiveness, love, and faith can and will serve to dramatically impact your life in a positive nature, leading you ever closer to the spiritual path that God has made available to you. If you can surrender to the omnipotent power, then you can resonate with the inexhaustible powers of the universe. Give in, don't give up. Work to maintain balance in all aspects of your life.

# Balancing Your Body with the Morter March

In keeping with your efforts to maintain balance, the Morter March was designed to be incorporated into your daily schedule. This simple and effective exercise will help to re-time your body. People who regularly perform this exercise report more flexibility, more energy, and a general feeling of "being more balanced." You need no special equipment or clothing to get started. Here's how it works.

Stand comfortably erect, remaining alert yet relaxed. Take an extended step with your left foot, keeping your back (right) foot firmly on the floor. Stretch just far enough forward with your left foot so that you can keep the heel of your back (right) foot on the floor.

As you extend your left leg, raise your right arm to about a forty-five degree angle. Your left arm will automatically move back to help you balance. Stretch your left arm downward behind you at about a forty-five degree angle. Your position at this point is left leg and right arm stretched forward, right leg and left arm stretched back.

Now, turn your head toward the side of the extended right

arm, look up, and s-t-r-e-t-c-h. While you are in your extended position, take a deep breath and hold it for as long as you can, while remaining in this position. Exhale and repeat the maneuver with the opposite leg and arm. Repeat this sequence three or four times—fewer if you become tired.

Do the Morter March workout twice a day. (I suggest starting your day and ending your day with this routine.) You may also do the exercise as a continuous motion—without holding your breath—at the beginning and end of any other regular exercise regimen. Two Morter March steps with each foot are enough. You will notice that the movements are exaggerations of a normal contralateral walk.

When you first attempt the Morter March, you may find that you have trouble balancing in your extended position. You can improve your stability by giving yourself a broader base on which to stand. Rather than putting one foot on a line directly in front of the other, widen your stance to suit your balance needs. You will probably notice improvement in your balance after doing this exercise regularly for a week or so. At that point, you can narrow your stance to fit your improved balance skills.

Make sure you do the Morter March with contralateral movement (extend right leg and left arm simultaneously and left leg with right arm simultaneously). Some people find that their initial inclination is to step out on one leg and have the arm on the same side follow. That is not the correct position for optimal results. In fact, extending both the arm and leg on the same side simultaneously may even result in the development of a headache, neckache, or such.

When done correctly, this simple exercise is very powerful in balancing your body. The length of time necessary for changes to become noticeable vary from person to person. Some people are reasonably healthy when they begin and may notice changes quickly. Others may not be so healthy and may not notice any difference for weeks or even months. The key to reaping the benefits of the Morter March is to perform the routine twice per day.

An added component to the Morter March would be to think positive affirmations as you hold your breath, while performing the exercise. The addition of positive thinking will increase the overall benefits. You might think, "Thank you for my perfect health," or, "I am becoming a better person everyday." The point is to think a positive thought or two. Not only will you re-time your body, but you will also reinforce the bond between your body and the field around you. While this will take only a few minutes each day, the results will be a tremendous help in balancing your spirit, soul, memory, mind, and body.

# Let Positive Thinking Replace Negative Thinking

I have made reference to this concept throughout this book, especially in the sections on the steps of forgiveness. It sounds so simple—replace negative thinking with positive thinking—yet we all know that this is not necessarily an easy task. Does this mean you should go around like a bubble-headed, bright-eyed, toy robot that always has a smile on its face? Does it mean that every time someone jerks the rug out from under you that you should think, "What a nice feeling"? Or that you should see the world through rose-colored glasses? Absolutely not. What I propose is not so shallow as any of that implies.

## SOUL PRINCIPLE

*The mind is never right but when it is at peace within itself; the soul is in heaven even while it is in the flesh, if it be purged of its natural corruptions, and taken up by divine thoughts and contemplations.*

—Seneca

What I do propose is that you realistically view and review the experiences of your life. For this way of thinking to be truly effective you must *believe* that you are actually better for having experienced each event. You must wholeheartedly *know* the good in the situation. When this occurs, you will be aware of it. You will actually feel as though your being has been enveloped with the knowledge. Some say they feel "lighter." Others report a sense of "peacefulness" or "calmness." I have even had people tell me that when they finally "got it," they felt like they had flipped a switch in their brain. Suddenly, the light came on and they understood the concept of "seeing the good in the situation."

Once you "get it," you will also accomplish the goal of learning the lesson. I believe that seeing the good in negative experiences is directly tied to learning the lesson of the event. The two go hand-in-hand. When you "get" one, you "get" the other. Each experience in your life is an opportunity to learn a lesson; the lesson is part of the good in the experience.

While many theologians, poets, political leaders, motivational speakers, authors, entrepreneurs, philosophers, and even talk-show hosts espouse the benefits of positive thinking, only *you* can make it a personal endeavor. Only you can take it upon yourself to replace your negative thoughts with positive ones. As I have said before, when you think positive thoughts, you create and put out positive information into your field. In this realm, likes attract. So, positive attracts positive and negative attracts negative. Now, given the choice, which would you choose? Negative or positive? I feel quite confident that the vast majority of you would choose to be surrounded in positive things.

You would most likely choose positive thoughts over negative ones and positive people over negative people. You would like to have positive, happy experiences, not negative, dreadful ones. The central notion to my way of thinking is that you understand that you have the ability within yourself to attract the objects and events you desire. This idea brings with it the fact that you may also bring about the negative thoughts that you put into your field of information. While this may seem out of your power, I assure you, it is real.

Your thoughts are a form of energy. A form of that spiritual, universal energy that we have discussed throughout this work. It is this same form of energy that created you and everything else in creation. The physical world, as we know it, originated from something that was not physical, something that did not have form.

Albert Einstein reports his strong inquisitiveness at watching the needle of a compass move when changing directions. He was obsessed with trying to figure out the force that moved the needle. This force is a form of energy. Can you see it without the compass needle? No. Is it still there without the compass needle? Absolutely. It is not a physical form, but it is an energy that is in all living things in this universe. It has a direct impact on objects—an attraction. In the field of magnetism, it is quite obvious and easy to see this attraction at work. We can't see the actual energy that does the pulling, but we can see the objects being pulled together. The energy force—God, universal intelligence—is there, repelling and attracting. It is everywhere, all the time. It is even within each of us.

## SOUL PRINCIPLE

*The more accurately we search into the human mind, the stronger traces we everywhere find of the wisdom of Him who made it.*

—Edmund Burke

While we cannot see the force within us, it is working all the time. In fact, the entire universe pulses with this energy force. The ocean tides move in and out accordingly. Your heart pulses and throbs. The wind rushes and subsides and all of God's creatures thrive and decline in accordance with this energy force. The solar system is in a state of perpetual motion. Everything on each planet is effected by this motion. Even though it is undetectable to us as we sit at our dinner tables, our earth is actually hurtling through space, with its moon orbiting, while spinning at a constant rate of speed. The gravitational pull is working all of the time to keep everything intact.

And rest assured that you are effected by this energy. It moves you and it moves within you. The energy that created the universe created you, and is in you as it is in the air around you. It is electrical and magnetic. It has the built-in quality of attraction. The beauty of it is that you can make this energy work for you, because it is a part of you.

As I discussed in Chapter 1, this universal energy can be harnessed to work *for* you. It is, in fact, working for you all the time, even if you do not realize it. If you are a positive thinker who makes good use of your time and good choices in the Six Essentials for Life, then you are more than likely reaping the benefits of good health, happiness, and success. You are actually attracting those rewards to you by your thoughts and your actions. On the other hand, if you are caught in a downward spiral of negative thinking and making poor choices in the six essentials, then you are probably living life in some degree of ill health or disease. And, in this instance, it may seem that Murphy's Law of "If something bad can happen, it will," has got you by the tail. One bad thing after another just "happens" to you. The opposite holds true for your optimistic, bright, shiny neighbor. Everything just seems to go her way.

Well, thus is life. This is the way of the universal, spiritual energy of nature. Positive attracts positive, while negative attracts negative. In order to collect on the positive side of things, you must change your way of thinking and acting. You may have to make a radical change in your lifestyle by changing the choices you make in many of the Six Essentials for Life. You may only need to make a small change in one or a few of the six essentials. Start with the one that will be the easiest and work toward the more challenging. Only you can recognize the necessary actions you must take. Only you can alter what you attract in the universe.

If you are uncertain whether you are thinking and emitting negative or positive, all you need to do is look around you. Are you surrounded by people who are loving, kind, gentle, and happy? Or are the people around you grouchy, angry, jealous, and resentful? The answer to this question is the answer to how you think and what you radiate from your field.

The first step in altering what you attract is to become aware of the fact that you can make a different life for yourself. You can attract health, wealth, happiness, and whatever else you so desire. You can bring things into your physical world by tapping into that universal energy source that is within you. You can learn to attract positive instead of negative by viewing the experiences in your life from the positive frame of mind. The physical world and the spiritual world are part of one harmonious whole when you make the right choices, live according to God's grand plan, and walk the path he paved.

# Peeling Off the Old Layers of Yourself

Once you begin to utilize the steps of forgiveness, replace negative thinking with positive thinking, and learn the lessons life offers you, you will find that self-examination of your past is automatic. Those who attend my health retreats often comment on this self-actualization process. They say they feel a need to use these new techniques to "clean up" their past experiences. By reviewing the past, seeing the good in each experience, learning the lesson, and replacing negative interpretations of the events with positive ones, you can do the same in your own life. Your health depends on you.

## SOUL PRINCIPLE

*When health is absent, wisdom cannot reveal itself, art cannot become manifest, strength cannot fight, wealth becomes useless, and intelligence cannot be applied.*
—Herophilus, physician of Alexandria

I have had many patients tell me that they sat down and started with their earliest negative experiences and worked through them one at a time up to the present—not in one sitting, but over time. It is much like peeling off the layers of an onion. Thin, dead fragments slide off the body quickly, while some of the thicker, tougher ones take a bit more effort. You will find that you have some events that you can easily and quickly neutralize with strong positive emotions. Then you will find that some of your past negative ordeals are more challenging to overcome. The good news is that you can and will succeed at doing so, if you stay with it. Continue to examine the situation until you can identify the good in it for you. Then you can replace the negative feelings you have about the experience with positive ones. You will have learned the lesson.

Another interesting aspect of working through past negative events is that you may find that you are able to neutralize or shed yourself of an event only to find that you begin to think about it again at a later date. You find that you once again feel the need to neutralize or overcome the negative emotions of the experience. That is quite common. It does not necessarily mean that you were unsuccessful the first time. Often the need to repeat the process of overcoming a negative experience is brought about by another situation that you are working through which is similar or related to the original event. It may also be triggered by an event that is currently taking place in your life, something that is similar or reminds you of the original and powerful negative emotions.

If this should happen to you, keep in mind that it happens to many of us. It is only necessary to go through the same steps of identifying the good, learning the lessons, and following the steps of forgiveness in order to take charge of the situation once again. The more traumatic the experience was, the more often you may find that you feel the need to follow the steps to overcome it. Just remember, you are in charge of your life from this point forward. You can peel off the old negative layers of yourself, revealing the shiny, new layers. This new you is a powerful, insightful being that utilizes the forces of universal energy. By using this energy to work for you, you are not taking away from the energy, but are actually fulfilling the laws of the spiritual world. You are completing the whole picture, walking in harmony with the one and true spiritual path. It is your use of this innate, spiritual power or energy that actually attracts the creative energy to you.

# Believe in Your Perfect Self

The ability to think and to use the free will instilled within you is a divine power. Recognition of this divine power is what human life is all about. The very notion that the universal energy that brought you and all of creation into being still resides within you supports an inner knowledge that is beyond compare. Furthermore, this universal energy is controllable by you and just waiting for your direction. This invisible, yet powerful, energy is the creator of the physical, mental, and spiritual realms. You can tap into and make use of this universal energy to create a healthy, positive, successful life for yourself or you can create thoughts and images that will attract negativity to you. The choice is yours.

This is not to say that you actually create the energy, but only that you *utilize* the perfect creative, universal energy that is within you and surrounding you. And it *is* perfect. It is omnipotent, divine, celestial, all-knowing, and almighty. Furthermore, it is always available to you. You have only to reach out into the universal consciousness to find it. As you utilize the information you may even add to it, thus replenishing and revitalizing the pool of wisdom and knowledge. By acknowledging the universal intelligence and using positive mental imaging to balance your experiences in life, you are actually working *with* the divine universal energy to accomplish your goals and assure your intentions.

You were created in the perfect image of the perfect energy; you are perfect in this sense. All you have to do is to allow the energy to work within you. You need time to grow and learn. You need to understand the concepts and work with these new techniques in order to fully flourish and attain success with them.

In Part I, I pointed out the necessity of becoming aware of the powers of the universe and recognizing that the powers reside within you and all of creation—*the Path of Enlightenment.* Then, in Part II, you learned that you must explore the universal intelligence or energy and how it works in the physical, mental, and spiritual planes—*the Path of Knowledge.* Finally, in Part III, you discover the need to move beyond belief, to actually *know* that you can tap into the powers of creation and put them to work for you in your daily life—*the Path of Fulfillment.*

It is knowing the universal energy or intelligence and applying it in your own life that can and will lead you to good health, happiness, and success. *Knowing* the power of your mind can set you free to become who you want to be. This knowledge will actually *assure* that you receive that which you desire. The key is to picture yourself exactly the way you want to become, see yourself as if you were already that way. Know that by doing this, you *are* that way. You have created it in the spiritual realm and it will come about in the physical. You are capable of good health, you can score high grades, your store can be number one in sales, you have met your professional goals, you are really happy, you will weigh your desired weight, or whatever you wish. The point is that you must *believe* this to be true, without doubt or fear. Beyond believing is knowing. And, always be thankful for all that you have!

## SOUL PRINCIPLE

*Belief consists in accepting the affirmations of the soul;*
*unbelief, in denying them.*

—Ralph Waldo Emerson

It is best to set aside a specific time to do mental imaging. Choose a time of day that you find you are most creative and will not be disturbed. I find that my best time for this is in the early morning hours, since I tend to get up before the world around me stirs. You may find morning a good time for you, too. Or you may prefer the lunch hour or just before bedtime. The key is to do some serious, deep mental imaging. Focus on seeing your goals already accomplished. *Believe* that you have succeeded in whatever you desire to achieve. As the old adage goes, "I see," said the blind man to his deaf son." It is possible to see without looking and hear without listening.

You can use affirmations to help you with this exercise, especially at first. You may want to write down your specific goal in the form of a positive statement. I call these the "I am" statements. You may have only a few "I ams" or you may have a long list. For instance, "I am the number one salesman on the team." "I am a perfect size eight." "I am in good health, with a perfectly functioning heart." The great thing about an "I am" is that you can personalize it to your specifications. During your mental imaging sessions, repeat your "I am" statements over and over. You may need to read them initially, but you will find that soon you are able to move through them without the need of your list.

Remember, the spiritual intelligence does not know time and space. So if you are not creating that which you desire, know that it has already been created in the spiritual world simply by your thinking it so. It may take more time to create it in the physical world. The frequency, dedication, and focus that you give your images is critical. Singleness of purpose never meant so much as in this instance. You cannot dictate, command, or order the universal intelligence. It does not work that way. In fact, it only works if you sufficiently and truly believe and have faith that it will work. Doubt, fear, and other such emotions work to negate the power of creation.

## SOUL PRINCIPLE

*He who doubts from what he sees*
*Will ne'er believe, do what you please.*
*If the Sun and Moon should doubt,*
*They'd immediately go out.*

—William Blake

It is only through your unique connection to and bond with God and the spiritual path that you can create and attract the positive "I am" statements to you. Your trust in this power is vital to your success in attracting the positive and valuable state that you desire, whether it be in health, your profession, your personal relationships with others, or any other facet of your life. If you question how you can attain that which you desire, then belief in the universal intelligence and that it resides within you and can be utilized by you is the answer. You must believe. In fact, you must take a step beyond belief. Let me explain what I mean by that.

# Journey of Knowingness

Belief, as defined by Webster, is: "a state or habit of mind in which trust or confidence is placed in some person or thing." Interestingly enough, Webster defines *know* as: "to be aware of the truth or factuality of: be convinced or certain of." Know, as a synonym, is defined like this:

"**syn** KNOW, BELIEVE, THINK *shared meaning element*: to hold something in one's mind as true or as being what it purports to be. These words are often used interchangeably with little thought of discrimination so as to convey quite distinct ideas. In such use KNOW stresses assurance and implies a sound logical or factual basis; BELIEVE, too, stresses assurance but implies trust and faith (as in a higher power) as its basis; while THINK suggests probability rather than firm assurance and implies mental appraisal of pertinent circumstances as its basis. Thus, 'I *know* he is telling the truth' implies such factual information in the hands of the speaker as fully confirms the questioned statement; 'I *believe* he is telling the truth' can imply such knowledge of the character and personality of the one challenged as to inspire perfect trust; 'I *think* he is telling the truth' implies no more than an acceptance of the probability of truthfulness in light of the circumstances."

The use of this definition helps me to clarify and distinguish between my concepts of belief and knowingness. The difference, to me, lies in the assured factual confirmation, without a trace of doubt, when you *know* something. Knowing goes beyond thinking or believing something to be true. It reaches a state of fact, that leaves no room for fear, doubt, or analysis. If you *know* it, it just is—no question, period.

This is the way I feel about the concepts that I have shared with you in this book. I *know* that they are true. I have been given this information and have worked to continue to develop my understanding of it for the past thirty-nine years. I know there is a super intelligence, a universal energy. Furthermore, I, like so many others, know that this force exists beyond a shred of doubt. It is my hope that you share this knowingness with me.

As I have said, this energy or intelligence has received many different titles—God, Buddha, chi, *prana*, life force, odic force, innate intelligence, creative force, universal energy, etc.—but the divine power remains a constant. Call it what you will. I only hope that you not only recognize it, but *know* that it exists. Remember, your title for it does not change it one bit. In fact, whether you even believe or know that it exists has no bearing at all on its existence.

Furthermore, I hope you *know* that this creative force resides within you and that you are capable of tapping into it for your own personal use. You can harvest the energy of your field. In fact, due to the nature of the energy, your thoughts, either positive or negative, actually attract the same into your field—without any effort on your part to do so. As I've said many times, positive thoughts and actions bring positive elements into your life, while negative produces and attracts negative.

Know that you are special and unique and that you were created by this ultimate energy source. Since you are part of the creation of this energy, it still resides within you; its powers are available to you. By simply applying the techniques I have outlined for you, you can have a dramatic and life-changing effect on your own life. The insight, application, and fulfillment of your dreams is available to you. All you need to do is reach out, open up, and give in to become one with this universal force of energy. I *know* this to be true. For your sake, I hope that you do, too.

I have endeavored to take you on a journey. A journey that began with the *Path of Enlightenment*. Remember, I stated early on that I cannot turn the power on within you, but I can certainly turn you on to the power. Our journey then moved through the *Path of Knowledge,* where we learned and explored how the presented concepts could and would effect you in your daily life. And, finally, we moved into this, the *Path of Fulfillment.* It is this path that is the ultimate goal. To become fulfilled is the epitome of the human dream. To be fulfilled means to bring to an end, to satisfy. It also means to convert into reality and to develop the full potentialities of something. Walking in harmony with the spiritual path, joining your soul and your spirit, is walking the path of fulfillment. It is now your responsibility to take an action step; after all, your health is *your* choice. It is my dream that you convert these principles into realities for you—that you reach into yourself to develop to your full potential. That is what God intended.

# Summary of Points

**PART I**

Chapter 1—The Powers Within You
* God gave us free will to choose and think with our conscious mind.
* We use our conscious mind to create our soul.
* Our spirit is the innate, divine, celestial, God force of the universe.
* Six Essentials for Life
    • What you eat and drink, how you exercise and rest, what you breathe and think.
    • Make good choices in each of these six areas.
    • What you think is the most important of all.

Chapter 2—Energy Fields
* We are surrounded by and contain fields of energy.
* Our soul and spirit are energy forces within us.
* Our energy fields control our bodies.
* We can utilize the energetic, spiritual force that created us to maintain health.
* We can create emotional memory override with our conscious mind. We an even create subconscious emotional memory override.
* The soul purpose in life is to attain and maintain harmony in soul and spirit.

**PART II**

Booster Thoughts
* The right choices in the Six Essentials for Life lead

to health, happiness, and success.

* You are in charge of your life and health.
* Choose to be nice, rather than right.
* Each day allows for a new beginning.
* Fear separates you from the universal power.
* Face your fears to overcome them.
* To judge is to rate something according to your own opinion or perception.
* Love more, expect less.
* God's love is unconditional.
* Give thanks for your ability to give and receive unconditional love.
* Three steps of forgiveness
  * Identify a situation, then:
    - Forgive yourself
    - Forgive the other person
    - Give the other person permission to forgive you
* Forgive for *you*, not for anyone else.
* To forgive does not mean to condone.
* Indecision can lead to disease.
* Beyond belief is "knowing."
* It is God's will that you be happy, healthy, and successful in life.
* What you think about, you bring about.
* God is perfect, all the time.
* Our thoughts, beliefs, and attitudes have no affect on God.
* Loneliness, or divine homesickness, is separation between soul and spirit.
* Pray as though you have already received that for which you pray.
* Meditate to reach your higher level of consciousness.
* Thoughts are silent prayers and all prayers are answered.

**PART III**

Chapter 6—Universal Consciousness
* Soul information and spirit information form universal consciousness.
* We take from and give to the universal consciousness.

Chapter 7—Practical Steps to a Healthy Life
* Your health is up to you.
* Rate yourself on your effective choices in the Six Essentials For Life.
* Be thankful for the perfect plan.
* Practice the steps of forgiveness.
* The Morter March will balance your body and mind.
* Replace negative thinking with positive thinking.
* Learn the lesson of the moment and from past experiences; see the *good* in them.
* Believe in the divine power and know that it resides within you.
* Move beyond belief into knowingness.
* Utilize the powers within you to reach your full potential.

# APPENDIX 2

# ENDNOTES

1   Jaffe, Lionel R., and Chaudio D. Stern. *Science*, Vol 211, March 13, 1981, p. 1147–1149.
2   Ibid, p. 1147–1149.
3   Cousens, Gabriel, M.D., as quoted in the introduction to *Vibrational Medicine*, (Gerber, Richard, M.D., Bear and Co.: Santa Fe, NM), p. 27–30.
4   Nakagawa, Kyoichi, M.D. (translation) *Japan Medical Journal*, No. 2745, December 4, 1976.
5   Hunt, Valerie V., as quoted on dust cover, *Infinite Mind*, (Malibu Publishing Co.: Malibu, CA, 1989).
6   Goldsmith, M., *Franz Anion Mesmer* (Doubleday: Garden City, NY, 1934).
7   Goetz, *The New Encyclopedia Britannica*, Vol. 27, p. 301.
8   Chopra, Deepak, M.D., *Quantum Healing: Exploring the Frontiers of Mind/Body Medicine*, (Bantam Books: New York, NY, 1989) p. 248.
9   Truman, Karol. K., *Feelings Buried Alive Never Die*, (Olympus Distribution: Las Vegas, NV, 1991), p. 177–202.
10  Justice, Blair, Ph.D., *Who Gets Sick* (Peak Press: Houston, TX, 1988) p. 84.
11  Lewis, H. Spencer, Ph.D., *The Secret Doctrines of Jesus* (Supreme Grand Lodge of Amore Printing and Publishing Department, 1971) p. 231.
12  Berg, Ragnar, and R.A. Richardson, as cited in Gayslord Hauser's *Be Happier, Be Healthier* (Farrar, Straus and Young: New York, NY) p. 139–141.
13  Ibid, p. 48–58.
14  Ibid, p. 48–58.
15  Lamm, Stephen, M.D., and Gerald Secor Couzens, as found in *Thinner At Last* (Simon and Shuster: New York, NY, 1995) p. 118.
16  Ibid, p. 118.
17  Ibid, Justice, *Who Gets Sick*, p. 120.
18  Finney, J.M.T. (1934) discussion of papers on shock, *Annals of Surgery*, 100, p. 746.
19  Miller, T.R. (1977) psychophysiologic aspects of cancer, *Cancer*, 39, p. 414.
20  Ibid, p. 113.
21  Hansen, Mark Victor and Jack Canfield, as quoted on back cover of *A 3rd Serving of Chicken Soup for the Soul* (Health Communications, Inc.: Deefield Beach, FL).
22  Jung, Carl, *Modern Man in Search of a Soul* (Harcourt Brace: New York, NY 1955).
23  Dyer, Wayne W., *Manifest Your Destiny*, (Harper Collins: New York, NY, 1997).
24  Ibid, Jung, *Modern Man in Search of a Soul*.
25  Watson, Lyall, as cited in *Beyond Supernature* (Hodder & Stoughton: London, 1986) p. 49–51.
26  Ibid, *Beyond Supernature*, p. 79–80.
27  Ibid, *Beyond Supernature*, p. 79–81.

# INDEX

alternative xii, 26, 47, 71, 72, 82
attitude 87, 88, 121, 123, 124; thoughts on, 46–122
belief xiv, xv, 47, 74, 85, 100, 114–115, 137, 143, 196–198; builders, 86, 136–137, 164–165; thoughts on, 116–122
believe xi, xiv, 1, 3–5, 8, 11–13, 16, 18–20, 23, 24, 28, 30, 34, 45, 46, 47, 48, 53, 87, 88, 89, 92, 94, 96, 109, 113–116, 118, 119, 120, 126, 131, 135, 156, 160, 162, 165, 184, 190, 197–199; perfect self, 195–198
body v, xv, 3, 4, 7, 9–19, 22–47, 55, 56, 58, 59, 60, 65, 67–79, 82, 86–88, 91, 92, 95, 102, 103, 112–114, 118–124, 128, 134, 135, 139, 148, 153, 161, 164, 165, 171, 173, 176–179, 186; balancing, 188–190
breathe xiii, xv, 21, 24, 28, 32–34, 82, 89, 120, 156, 176, 178, 179, 182; thoughts on, 66–69
conscious xi, xvi, 7–9, 13, 15, 20–22, 29, 30, 31, 34, 36–39, 47, 49, 50, 67, 72, 82, 140, 142, 144, 151, 152
consciousness 31, 48, 53, 78, 83, 85, 139–144, 153, 154, 156–158, 161–165, 180, 196; universal, 169–179
create xvi, 8, 9, 10, 16, 18, 31, 39, 41, 46, 48, 50, 53– 55, 56, 58, 83–85, 121, 146, 171, 186, 191, 196
creative 35, 64, 83, 135, 136, 152
eat xiii, xv, 14, 20, 21, 22, 23, 24, 26–36, 42, 82, 88, 90, 120, 160, 171, 176, 181; thoughts on, 56–66
emotional xv, 10, 15, 17, 36, 41, 42, 43, 44, 46, 49, 74–76, 87, 92, 93, 107, 112, 113, 151, 178, 185
emotions xv, 8, 10, 16, 17, 30, 36, 37, 39, 41, 42, 44, 45, 46, 47, 74– 77, 80, 151, 165, 194, 195
energy ix, xv, 3–6, 9–19, 24, 32, 34–36, 45–48, 53, 56, 67, 70–76, 77, 83–86, 91, 93–95, 103, 104, 107, 113–126, 129, 131–136, 139, 142, 147, 152–156, 161–165, 169, 173, 174, 178, 188, 193, 195, 196; fields, 15–18
enlightenment 1, 108, 109, 120, 130, 196; path of, 1–50
exercise xiii, xv, 21, 26–31, 33, 37, 55, 67, 68, 69, 82, 120, 176, 177, 182; thoughts on, 70–74
experience xi–xvi, 9, 15, 17, 22, 24, 28, 38, 41, 42, 48, 49, 75, 76, 90, 91, 92, 100, 102, 107–110, 114, 117, 121, 124, 125, 127, 133, 136, 144, 145, 150, 151, 178–179, 185, 190, 194, 195
faith 4, 84–85, 93, 100, 103, 131, 139; thoughts on, 140–145
fear xv, 37–42, 44–46, 75, 79, 89, 100, 101, 106, 122, 131, 132, 134, 143,

fear (cont.) 171; thoughts on, 91–95
feelings xi, 8, 36, 37, 39, 42, 46, 47, 49, 80, 83–88, 95, 100–102, 107, 110, 111, 113, 122–126, 130, 131, 135, 151, 164, 171, 185, 194
field xv, 20, 34, 36, 87, 100, 101, 103, 104, 118, 119, 122, 123, 124, 125, 126, 130, 142, 146, 147, 164, 171, 173; energy of, 15–18; health, 10–15
forgiveness 48, 76, 100, 122, 136–137, 165, 184, 185, 194, 195; steps to, 184–186; thoughts on 107–111
fulfillment xiv, 102, 114; path of, 167–200
future xiv, 19, 71, 86, 94, 122, 125, 147, 179
God xiii, xv, 3, 4, 5, 7, 21, 36, 42, 48, 49, 51, 77, 78, 85, 88, 94, 99, 101–104, 115– 122, 129, 130–135, 139–142, 144, 146–156, 159, 161, 162, 164, 169, 171, 172, 175, 186, 198
happiness xvi, 8, 10, 44, 53, 73, 118, 136, 140, 164; thoughts on, 88–91
harvest 15, 16, 18, 164; energy field, 15–18
healing 3, 12, 15, 18, 94, 97, 102, 129
health v, xi, xiv, xv, xvi, 5, 8, 16, 17, 18, 20, 53, 54, 55, 56, 59, 60, 64, 66, 70–76, 95, 101, 102, 106, 107, 108, 112, 113, 116, 118, 119, 121, 124, 136, 139, 140, 141, 145, 164, 171, 178, 183, 184, 185; field of, 10–15; thoughts on disease, 79–86
healthy ix, xv, xvi, 11, 59, 60, 71, 74, 77, 89, 91, 106, 117, 118, 119, 123, 150, 151, 175, 183, 186, 196
indecision 46,; thoughts on, 111–116
innate xv, 6, 7, 8, 12, 19, 20, 32, 37, 38, 40, 46, 47, 48, 50, 82, 116, 136, 139, 152, 154, 161, 170, 195
interference 17, 20, 34, 76, 77, 84, 85, 109, 112, 130, 132, 134, 135
journey xiv, 85, 112, 141, 149; knowing-ness, 198–200
judge 40, 90, 91, 96, 97, 101, 121, 124, 137, 140, 165
judgment 46, 100, 101, 103, 114, 115, 116, 124, 137, 143, 145, 178; thoughts on, 96–99
know xi, xiii, xiv, xvii, 5, 9, 12, 18, 22, 27, 28, 29, 32, 36, 39, 44, 48, 53, 87, 89, 90, 93, 94, 96, 99, 102, 104, 108, 110, 111, 115, 116, 120, 122, 125, 128, 129, 131–135, 151, 165, 190, 196, 199
knowingness xvi, 85, 93, 114, 116, 143; journey, 198–200
knowledge xiv, 45, 47, 49, 170, 171, 196; path of, 51–166
kudu 157, 158
learn 85, 140, 143, 145, 171, 178–179

lesson 18, 23, 88, 94, 95, 96, 108, 109, 122, 125, 136, 137, 139, 143, 145, 184, 185, 194
loneliness xv, 8, 38, 40, 42, 46, 94, 101, 102; thoughts on, 126–135
love 42, 44, 48, 58, 71, 85–88, 91, 97, 130, 133, 134, 135, 137, 142, 149, 151, 162, 164, 186, 188; thoughts on, 99–106
master program 7, 8, 9, 10, 12, 13, 19, 20, 30, 32, 33, 40, 41, 42, 45, 68, 120, 139, 154
medicine xiii, 13–15, 31, 39, 48, 79; preventative, 180–183
memory 31, 36–37, 40, 41, 42, 43, 44, 46, 56, 75, 77, 87, 92, 107, 109, 131, 150, 178, 186
mental xv, 15, 30, 41, 42, 44, 46, 54, 70, 72–75, 76, 85, 145, 196; plane, 87–138
mind v, xiv, xv, xvi, 3, 4, 7, 8, 9, 10, 13, 15, 16, 17, 20, 21, 56, 68, 73, 76, 77, 79, 87, 88, 91, 93, 94, 95, 96, 102, 103, 107, 110, 111, 112, 115, 118, 119, 121, 134, 136, 137, 140, 142, 152, 176; matters, 21–50
negative 11, 34, 36, 39, 41, 44, 45, 47, 49, 64, 75, 76, 77, 80, 82, 83, 87, 94, 95, 96, 100–104, 107, 110, 112, 113, 115, 121, 123, 134–136, 157, 164, 171, 172, 185, 194; thinking, 190–193
override 75, 76, 87, 107, 178; emotional memory, 36–47
past 30, 33, 42, 46, 107, 109, 110, 112, 114, 115, 121, 122, 124, 130, 147, 179
path 1, 8, 9, 10, 85, 89, 100, 104, 109, 114, 122, 136, 144, 148, 149, 152, 153, 156, 160, 167, 173, 176; knowledge, 51–66; spiritual walking, 47–50
perfect xv, 6, 7, 8, 23, 24, 27, 38, 40, 41, 47, 50, 89, 99, 101, 104, 109, 113, 116, 117, 118, 119, 120, 121, 136, 139, 147, 148, 171, 176, 186; self, 195–198; thoughts on self, 159–164
physical v, xiii, xv, 10, 12, 13, 14, 15, 18, 24, 26, 28, 29, 34, 36, 38, 40, 41, 44, 45, 46, 47, 54, 92, 93, 102, 107, 110–114, 119, 120, 121, 134, 144, 145, 146, 153, 154, 162, 173, 186, 196; plane, 55–86
plane 15, 44, 55, 75, 87, 88, 90, 101, 102, 113, 134, 136, 139, 143, 162; mental, 87–138; physical, 55–86; spiritual, 139–166
positive 11, 31, 36, 47, 69, 73, 76, 77, 78, 80, 82, 83, 84, 85, 87, 88, 93, 94, 95, 96, 101–104, 115, 119, 121, 122, 123–126, 129, 134, 136, 147, 157, 164, 186, 194; thinking, 190–193
power xiv, xvi, 21, 30, 41, 45, 47, 48, 49, 50, 53, 85, 89, 91, 93, 94, 96, 101–104, 110, 114–116, 118, 120, 129,

power (cont.) 130–135, 139–142, 147, 153, 155, 161, 169, 186, 187, 191, 195; within, 3–20
prayer 14, 31, 48, 77, 78, 93, 103, 115, 117, 130, 139, 141, 164; proper, 186–188; thoughts on, 145–149
present 19, 95, 97, 106, 109, 122, 124, 130
preventative 180–183
program 7, 8, 9, 10–13, 19, 20, 27, 28, 29–33, 40, 41, 42, 45, 46, 71, 74, 120
reactions 75, 113, 124, 126, 178, 184
relationships, thoughts on, 122–126
rest xiii, xv, 15, 19, 21, 30, 31, 33, 36, 40, 41, 55, 82, 90, 101, 105, 120, 129, 131, 133, 176, 178, 182; thoughts on, 74–78
Six Essentials xiii, xv, 21, 22–36, 56, 82, 83, 120, 175–176, 179–181, 183, 193
sleep xv, 30, 31, 34, 41, 69, 74, 75–78, 87, 146, 177, 178, 182
soul xi, xii, xv, xvi, 5, 10, 14–17, 19, 20, 22, 33–36, 47, 53, 56, 73, 77, 78, 88, 90, 94, 95, 97, 100–104, 109, 113, 115, 118, 119, 122, 123, 124, 129–135, 137, 139, 142, 156, 169, 173, 176; differentiate, 170–172; introduction, 6–9; thoughts on integration, 149–153
space 18–20, 139
spirit xv, xvi, 10, 12, 15, 16, 17, 19, 20, 32, 33, 41, 46, 47, 50, 53, 56, 68, 73, 77, 88, 89, 90, 91, 93, 94, 95, 97, 99, 100–104, 114, 115, 118, 120–123, 130, 139, 142, 146, 147, 154, 155, 157, 160–163, 173, 187; differentiate, 170–172; introduction, 6–9; original, 169–170; thoughts on integration, 149–153
spiritual xv, 34, 38, 40, 46–50, 54, 77, 78, 83–85, 89, 90, 91, 94, 95, 100–104, 109, 113, 115, 116, 121, 122, 129, 131, 135, 136, 169, 170–173, 176, 186, 193, 195, 196; plane, 139–166; universal connection, 153–159
subconscious 7, 8, 9, 15, 23, 30, 32, 37, 38, 40, 43, 45, 54, 68, 75, 77, 78, 87, 93, 107, 112, 113, 131, 158, 159, 178
success xvi, 8, 10, 53, 70, 71, 73, 86, 88, 89, 94, 95, 101, 140
thankful 85, 90, 91, 94, 107, 109, 119, 121, 133, 148, 162–164, 178, 185, 186–188
think xiii, xv, xvii, 5–10, 12, 21, 23, 31, 34–38, 40–43, 46, 50, 55, 59, 64, 69–73, 79, 82, 86–90, 93, 96–100, 104, 107–113, 116–125, 131, 133–137, 141, 143, 156, 165, 176, 178, 179, 183, 199
universal 6, 19, 53, 54, 70, 83, 86, 91, 93, 94, 95, 99, 103, 104, 114, 139, 142, 144, –154, 164, 165, 195, 196; consciousness, 169–174; thoughts on spiritual connection,153–159